Cookbook

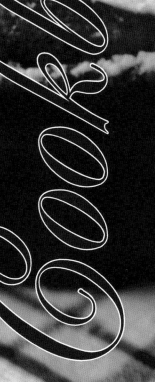

Suzanne's
Signature Dishes

elcome to my Signature Dishes. Cooking is one of my greatest Loves in my life and there are several reasons I have decided to create this cookbook.

When I serve family and friends my dishes they always asked me if they can have a copy of my recipes. Only one problem, I never used recipes to create my dishes so I did not have any recipes to give them. Subsequently, I have never developed a habit of having the same old meals night after night because I would consistently dream up new creations. I would simply dream up a new dish and I would go about creating it. I was never in the habit of measuring ingredients because when you are creating something a little of this and a little of that creates these wonderful dishes. My family would ask for a dish we had a month ago and I would not remember what I fed them exactly. So I finally came to the conclusion that I would need to start writing everything down that I did in the kitchen to create these dishes.

My goal is to do something with my life that will have a positive impact on society, and I wish to do this by sharing my gift and culinary creations with others. I believe so strongly in this idea that I will be donating the profits made from this cookbook to charity. I love to cook because I was taught this was a great way to show my love and appreciation to others. During the creation of this cookbook, I have documented my dishes by taking beautiful full-color photographs, and detailed measurements of required ingredients. I hope this cookbook will inspire you to want to create new, delicious meals for your family and friends and to enjoy them for years to come.

A special thank you to:

Cindy Brown for being my top recipe tester

and all those that helped test my recipes

Mary Ellis for your inspiration of photography

Suzanne Davis for her long time support

My husband Todd for all his love and support

ISBN: 0615383386
ISBN-13: 9780615383385

Table of Contents

Brunch & Bread

Appetizers

Soup & Salads

Vegetables

Pasta, Rice & Grains

Quinoa (KEEN-Wah) Pg. 69

Basil Pesto Rice Pg. 71

Grilled Mushroom & Asparagus Risotto Pg. 73

Beef Cannelloni Pg. 75

Baked Ziti Pg. 77

Homemade Pesto Pasta Pg. 78

Fish & Seafood

Chilean Sea Bass With Orange Sauce Pg. 83

Fillet Of Cod With A Pesto Crust Pg. 85

Alaskan Halibut With A Compote Sauce Pg. 86

Puff Pastry Wrapped Salmon Pg. 89

Parmesan Dill Crusted Baked Steelhead Trout Pg. 91

Citrus Baked Tilapia Pg. 93

Meat & Poultry

Desserts

Everything Else

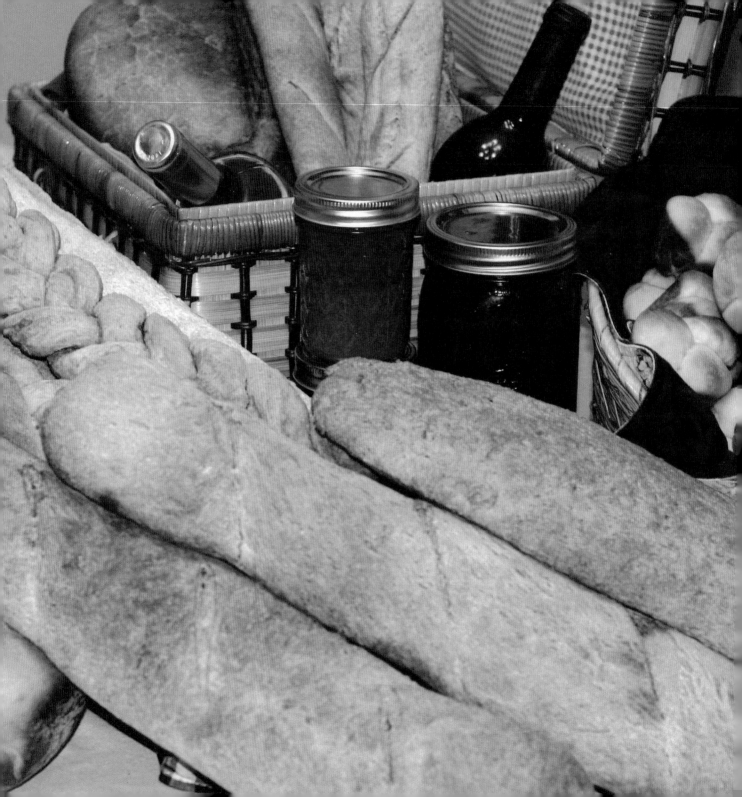

Brunch
&
Bread

Suzanne Schwendiman

BROCCOLI CHEESE SOUP OMELET

1-2 servings
Prep time: 10 minutes Total time: 15 minutes

What gives this omelet it's unique flavor is that the broccoli cheese soup is in the egg mixture to give it a light, fluffy, broccoli, cheese flavor stuffed with your favorite grilled vegetables.

One Omelet:
1 large egg
1/3 Cup liquid egg whites
1/4 Cup Homemade Broccoli Soup
(Recipe under Soup & Salad)

Optional Ingredients:
grilled portabella mushroom sliced
roasted red pepper sliced
5 black olives sliced
3 oz sauté spinach
4 sliced artichokes packed in water
1 oz goat cheese crumbled

Spray a preheated medium sauté pan (medium to high heat) with a nonstick spray. Whisk together egg, egg whites and soup until well incorporated. Pour into the preheated pan let omelet set up about 1 minute and with rubber Teflon spatula pick up sides of omelet with spatula and tilt the pan so the top can run off underneath of set omelet part, continue on all sides until omelet is soft set.

At this time spread on your favorite grilled vegetables and more cheese if desired. I suggest grilled portabella mushrooms, red peppers, black olives, spinach, artichokes and goat cheese makes a nice combo. Whatever you like even spread a little poached salmon into the omelet before cooking. There are endless combinations that can go into this uniquely made omelet.

Garnish with sour cream or plain Greek yogurt and fresh herbs such as chives, parsley or basil, etc.

NOTES: *This recipe was inspired from my love of making omelets.*

Suzanne Schwendiman

SPINACH & SALMON QUICHE

6-8 servings
Prep time: 10 minutes Total time: 1 hour

Spinach, eggs, cheese, salmon plus my homemade mustard dill sauce added in to give it a savory flavor.

Preheat oven 350° F (175° C).

Poach salmon on the stove in a medium sauce pan with hot boiling water to cover salmon, add one lemon zest and juiced, plus 3 slices of ginger (1/2" thick) until salmon flakes about 3-5 minutes. Place drained, flaked salmon along with spinach, eggs, egg whites, mozzarella, ricotta, parmesan cheese, onions, garlic, lemon/zest, mustard sauce and parsley into a large mixing bowl. Mix well by hand to incorporate the ingredients about 1-2 minutes. Place the pie crust into a greased deep 10" pie dish. (picture was made with tart pan) To form a prettier pie crust pinch the crust on edge all the way around. Pour quiche mixture into pie crust/pan and put into a preheated oven for about 55-60 minutes until top is puffed and set with a slight brown crust. Using a knife insert into center to see if it comes out clean. If crust becomes too brown place aluminum foil around edge to keep it from burning.

Remove from oven and place on wire rack to cool. Cut and serve warm with a dollop of sour cream or plain Greek yogurt and garnish with chives or minced peppers or tomato salsa. This quiche goes nicely with a salad, whole wheat baguette or even potato leek soup.

1 pie shell crust 10" deep dish

10 oz chopped frozen spinach (thawed, drain excess water)

5 large eggs

6 liquid egg whites

8 oz Fat Free shredded mozzarella

16 oz Low Fat ricotta cheese

1/2 Cup Parmesan cheese

4 green onions minced

1 Tbsp minced garlic

2 lemons juiced plus zest

3/4 Cup of mustard dill sauce (see recipe in the chapter entitled Everything Else)

12 oz poached salmon (one lemon juiced plus zest, 3 slices ginger root in boiling hot water until meat flakes)

1/4 Cup chopped parsley

Suzanne Schwendiman

NUTTY CRUNCHY WHOLE WHEAT BAGUETTES

3 Large Baguettes
Prep time: 15 minutes Total time: 2 1/2 hours

Coarsely ground white wheat gives the bread a nutty crunchy texture that is so good.

Combine dry ingredients into a large bowl of a standing mixer fitted with a dough hook. Turn your mixer on low and pour the maple syrup into the water and pour water mixture into bowl for about 4 minutes to form dough carefully scraping down sides of bowl to incorporate the flour. Cover the bowl and place in a warm place to rise for about 1 hour (I usually put mine in the microwave oven). If you like you can mix ingredients with a wooden spoon until it forms dough and then knead the dough on a well floured surface for about 5-10 minutes by hand until a smooth surface appears on dough, then let the dough rise until double in size.

4 Cups fresh <u>coarsely</u> ground white wheat

2 Tbsp vital wheat gluten

2 Cup unbleached all purpose white flour

1 Tbsp salt

1 Tbsp instant yeast or 2 packets of rapid rise yeast

16 oz warm water 110° F (43° C)

6 Tbsp Grade B Maple Syrup (Grade B is the second tap from the maple tree and has a richer and more intense maple flavor good for baking)

Divide dough into thirds about (1 lb each), shape dough into flattened oval, fold the dough in half lengthwise, and seal the edges with the heal of your hand. Flatten slightly, fold lengthwise, and seal again.

With the seam side down, cup your fingers and gently roll the dough into a 15" log. Place the log seam side down on to a lightly greased parchment lined baking sheet, or into the well of lightly greased baguette pan. Repeat for the other 2 pieces of dough.

Cover with plastic wrap and let rise till the baguette is very puffy, about 1 hour. Towards the end of the rising time, preheat your oven to 400° F (205° C).

Slash the baguette three or four times on the diagonal with a wet sharp knife or razor blade. Spritz heavily with warm water, and bake until a very deep golden brown, 20 to 25 minutes. Remove from the oven and cool on a rack.

NOTE: *You can shape dough into whatever shape you like; I even braided my baguette or put 2 pieces into refrigerator for another day. Also for the bread to have that nutty crunchy taste you will need to have very course ground white wheat and the maple syrup because that is what gives the bread that nutty crunchy taste.*

SOUR DOUGH STARTER:

2 Cups of bread flour (preferred is ground soft white wheat)
2 Cups of beer, mild flavored lager beer or mild non-alcoholic lager beer, contains flavor compounds similar to those in a dough starter, which gives the bread a taste boost), or (2 Cups warm water plus 1 envelope yeast and 1 tsp sugar)

Combine flour and whatever your liquid choice is in a plastic bowl and stir with a plastic or wooden spoon until it forms a thick liquid paste. Cover loosely with plastic lid leave on counter and stir once a day (if batter becomes too thin, add more flour and combine until paste is formed again). It will have a foul smell and may have a grey appearance to it when it is ready to use (**about 72 hours or up to a week**) but if batter is not being fed or used for a long time (more than 2 weeks) store in refrigerator with lid on. Always keep a cup from prior starter to mix in the new sour dough starter batch to keep starter going.

OLD WORLD SOUR DOUGH BREAD

YIELDS 2 POUND LOAF

Artisan bread that has a sweet sour taste with a perfect airy crumb soft center and firm golden crust that keeps you coming back for more.

Combine all dry ingredients in a large plastic bowl whisk together to incorporate the dry ingredients. Next add your wet ingredients and using a rubber spatula mix until sticky dough is formed about 3-4 minutes. Cover the bowl and put into a warm place for about 1 hour until it doubles in size.

On a floured surface knead dough for about 3 minutes and shape into a boule. Let rise in a large bowl (about 10 in") lined with parchment paper. Spray paper with oil and also spray dough with oil. Cover loosely with plastic wrap until doubled in size about 1 hour (for a professional looking top slice the dough with a razor or very sharp knife one 6" long, 1/2" deep slit along top of dough).

Heat oven to 450° F (230° C). Place pizza stone or enameled cast iron Dutch oven (6-8 quart) into oven for 30 minutes. (Dutch oven is the preferred method because as the loaf heats it gives off steam to create a very humid environment inside the Dutch oven; Since moist air transfers heat much more efficiently than dry air , the loaf heats much more rapidly causing the air bubbles inside to expand much faster leading to a more open crumb structure) Reduce oven temperature to 400° F (205° C). Carefully pick up parchment paper with dough and transfer to pizza stone or to your Dutch oven (top removed before dough is place into it and top placed back on for 30 minutes then top removed to brown the top of bread crust for another 5 minutes until it is golden brown) and mist the top of the bread with a milk and water mixture just before closing the oven to cook. Cook the bread for 30 minutes or until golden brown.

1 3/4 Cup warm water 110° F (43° C)

1 to 2 Cups of sourdough starter depending on how sour you like your bread (see recipe on page 8)

3 to 4 Cups bread flour or preferred method is fresh ground soft white wheat plus 2 Tbsp Vital Wheat Gluten

4 Tbsp white sugar or preferred is honey

2 Tbsp extra virgin olive oil

1 Tbsp salt

1 Tbsp of dry active yeast or 2 packet of instant yeast (follow direction on packet to dissolve if you desire)

Cool and serve with your favorite honey butter, jams or just simply with olive oil.

SWEET & SOUR CINNAMON CHIP BREAD

2 Pound loaf
Prep time: 15 minutes Total time: 3 hours

Light and fluffy texture with a sweet and tangy rich taste. Cinnamon chips spread generously throughout, along with some beautiful cinnamon swirls.

Place all dry ingredients (flour, sugar, salt) into a large plastic bowl whisk together until well incorporated. Using a rubber spatula or wooden spoon mix in the wet ingredients (starter, vanilla, beaten egg, melted butter and proof yeast and water a little at a time) for about 3-4 minutes until ingredients are well combined and you have a wet sticky dough formed. Cover bowl and let dough rest in a warm place for about 1 hour until doubled in size. Pour wet dough out on a floured surface and Knead in the 1 Cup of flour a little at a time then fold or knead the frozen chips a little at a time into dough until well incorporated through the loaf. Shape the dough into a boule and place back into same bowl lined with parchment paper that has been heavily sprayed with oil so the dough will not stick. Cover and place back into the warm area and let rise for about 1 hour or doubled in size. Half way through rise preheat oven to 400° F or 205° C with Dutch oven plus the lid or pizza stones into oven for 30 minutes then turn oven down to 375° F or 190° C. Carefully pick up the dough that has doubled in size by the overlapping parchment paper and put in to Dutch oven or on the pizza stone that has been preheat with oven. Cook the bread for about 30 minutes and uncover the Dutch oven and brown the top for about 10 minutes, if using the pizza stone the internal temp should read 200° F or 95° C by sticking a meat thermometer into the bottom of the loaf.

NOTES: *Makes a great French toast with your favorite maple syrup poured on top along with some unsalted butter.*

1 Cup of Sour dough Starter (see sour dough bread recipe)

1 1/2 Cups warm water 110 F (43° C)

4 tsp pure vanilla

1 large egg beaten

1/4 Cup melted unsalted butter

1 Tbsp salt

1 Cup sugar

1 Tbsp dry active yeast or 2 packets of rapid rise yeast (proof yeast)

4 Cups sifted all purpose unbleached white flour plus 1 Cup more for kneading into dough

10 oz frozen mini cinnamon chips dusted with flour

Suzanne Schwendiman

GOLDEN YELLOW CORNBREAD

10-12 Servings
Prep time: 10 minutes Total time: 1 hour

Warm, moist and sweet delicious flavor with coarse ground yellow corn. Good anytime of the day.

Preheat oven to 425° F (220° C).

Whisk together dry ingredients into bowl, add beaten eggs, milk, oil, honey and vanilla. Using an electric mixer beat until smooth and well incorporated about 1 minute on high. Do not over-beat.

Bake in a greased 9"x13" glass pan for about 25 – 30 minutes. Bake until center is firm and the inserted knife comes out clean.

Serve warm with honey butter.

It even tastes great with warm cream/milk poured on top.

Tip: There are many flavor combinations that can be added into the cornbread batter; For a breakfast muffin flair right before you put into oven mix into batter 1/2 cup of chopped caramelized onions, plus 1/2 cup of real crispy crumbled bacon, then pour into sprayed muffin tins and bake for about 12-15 minutes until toothpick inserted into center comes out clean and top springs back.

2 Cups fresh coarse ground yellow corn

2 Cups ground whole wheat pastry flour

1 tsp salt

8 tsp baking powder

1 Tbsp brown sugar

2 large eggs beaten

2 Cups Buttermilk <u>or</u> mix 2 Tbsp of white vinegar into 2 Cups of whole milk

3/4 Cup Extra Virgin Organic Coconut Oil

3/4 Cup honey

3 tsp pure vanilla

NOTES: *I never tasted cornbread that I liked before so I decided to make my own and see if I could make it taste better. Now I cannot stop making and eating this bread.*

BED & BREAKFAST ORANGE MUFFINS

24 Large or 48 Mini Muffins
Prep time: 20 minutes Total time: 35 minutes

Muffins with a sweet orange flavor that has an orange cake crumbled topping.
These muffins can be served with a cup of fresh fruit and yogurt on top.

Preheat oven to 350° F (175° C) and place rack in center of oven. The preferred method is to line muffin cups with paper/ foil cup liners or spray with a nonstick spray muffin pan that has 24 medium molds or 48 miniature muffin molds.

In a separate bowl, sift together to combine the flour, salt, baking soda and baking powder. Set aside.

In the bowl of your electric mixer, or hand mixer, cream the butter and sugar until light fluffy (about 2 minutes). Add the eggs one at a time until each egg is well incorporated. Scrape down the sides of the bowl and then beat in the buttermilk, orange extract, orange zest plus juice. Add the flour mixture 1/3 batch at a time until well incorporated.

Fill the prepared muffin tins almost full by using a spoon or a 1/4 measuring cup. Combine the topping ingredients together with a whisk until well incorporated. Sprinkle orange crumb topping over the top of each muffin with a teaspoon.

Bake for 15 to 20 minutes or until lightly browned and toothpick inserted into the center of a muffin comes out clean. (Length of baking time will depend on the size and color of the muffin tins used.)

Serve warm with fruit or cut in half and spread some of my peach marmalade on muffin (see recipe in the chapter entitled Everything Else).

Tip: Coconut flour can be found on line or in your local health food stores. You may also use dried sweetened coconut flakes in the food processor until ground fine (you air dry the coconut flakes, or place in an oven on 200° F until dried not toasted or in a dehydrator). You may use 3 cups of all purpose flour if you do not want to use coconut flour.

Muffin Batter:

2 Cup all purpose white flour

1 Cup Coconut Flour

1 tsp salt

2 tsp baking soda

2 tsp baking powder

3/4 Cup (170 grams) unsalted butter room temperature

1 1/4 Cup granulated white sugar

2 large eggs

1 Cup buttermilk

2 tsp orange oil extract

1 Tbsp orange zest plus juice from 2 large tangerine or 4 small tangerines

Orange Crumb Topping:

1 Cup sugar

1 Tbsp orange zest

2 slices 1" thick of store bought vanilla pound cake crumbled

2 tsp cinnamon

NOTES: *Inspired because of a dream of owning a bed and breakfast someday.*

DINNER ROLLS

(COCONUT OR ORANGE OR MAPLE)

24 Rolls
Prep time: 15 minutes Total time: 2 hours

These rolls are airy and light with a warm sweet taste of home. These scrumptious rolls can be coconut, orange or maple by mixing in one of the sweet flavor combinations. They are even great plain with a little bit of sweet honey drizzled down the sides. They are so versatile that they are truly great with any meal!

Main Ingredients:

2 packets rapid rise yeast

1 tsp sugar

1/4 Cup warm water

(110° F or 43° C)

Mix first 3 Main ingredients together in a large Bowl and set aside for about 10 minutes.

Add 1/2 Cup white sugar

3 large beaten eggs

2 tsp salt

1 Cup warm water 110° F (43° C)

5 Cups sifted all-purpose unbleached flour

plus more for dusting surface

Coconut Ingredients:

1/2 Cup minced sweeten coconut

1 Cup unsweetened Coconut Milk

(instead of 1 Cup warm water)

Maple Ingredients:

1/2 Cup Grade B Maple Syrup

(Instead of 1/2 Cup sugar)

1 oz maple extract

Orange Ingredients:

1 oz orange extract

1 medium-large orange juiced plus zest placed in 1 Cup measuring cup and top off with warm water to equal 1 Cup (instead of 1 Cup of warm water)

Continued on page 18

Mix main ingredients plus one of the flavor combinations if you desire into soft sticky dough but do not knead as you normally do making bread. Instead use a wooden spoon or dough scraper to handle and process dough, or oil hands. Let rise until double in size. Push dough down and maybe place in a refrigerator for up to 24 hours. Knead the dough on a well flour surface until a soft crust forms (about 2 min) and then you may roll out the dough on a well floured surface and make whatever style rolls you want. I usually roll out the dough to about 1/2" thickness and cut out with a 3" round cutter. Fold over the circle or cut out and press the front side down so that the roll will not open up while baking. Place on a baking sheet pan sprayed with oil and loosely cover with plastic wrap. Let rise about an hour or until double in size. It will take longer if you have had the dough in the refrigerator.

Bake rolls at 400° F (205° C) for about 7-10 minutes or until golden brown. Pour honey on rolls when they come out of oven if desired.

TIP: Coconut rolls can be served with a ham dinner, Orange rolls with a roasted duck or hen, Maple rolls can be served with any kind of sausage or a roasted turkey.

NOTES: *Originally inspired from an old friend and everyone loved these rolls.*

Appetizers

SPINACH CRAB DIP

4 Cups
Prep time 5 minutes Total Time: 45 minutes

This dip is like a fondue of jack cheese, creamy spinach and crab blended together.
The dip goes so well served with crostini.

1 dry pack of ranch dip

3/4 Cup mayonnaise

3/4 Cup sour cream

10 oz frozen chopped Spinach thawed/drained

16 oz imitation crab meat or fresh

4 Cups Monterrey jack cheese

1 baguette sliced/toasted

Preheat oven to 350° F (175° C).

Mix first six ingredients in a bowl then pour into a greased oven proof baking dish and bake for about 45 minutes until bubbling hot.

Serve warm with toast for dipping.

NOTES: *Inspired for my love of hot dips.*

PISA DIP

4 Cups
Prep time: 5 minutes Total time: 35 minutes

Irresistible bubbling hot fondue dip that tastes and smells like pizza.
Serve with crusty cubed bread for dipping into like a fondue pot.

3/4 Cup real mayonnaise	**1 tomato, seeded diced**
12 oz chopped pepperoni	**10 hot pepper rings finely chopped**
1/2 lb shredded Mozzarella cheese	**8 black olives minced**
1/2 lb shredded Smoked provolone Cheese	**1 loaf crusty bread cubed**

Preheat oven 350° F (175° C).

Mix all ingredients in a bowl then pour into an oven proof baking dish and bake for about 30 minutes until bubbling hot.

Serve with cubed bread for dipping.

NOTES: *Inspired from an old friend.*

Suzanne Schwendiman

BROCCOLI CHEESE ROLL

8 Servings
Prep time: 10 minutes Total time: 45 minutes

Hot delicious broccoli rolled up in a baked bread log with melted mozzarella, smoked provolone and parmesan cheese and served up as crusty hot round slices.

Preheat oven 375° F (190° C).

Spray cookie sheet pan with cooking spray, line the cookie sheet pan with parchment paper and spray with cooking spray again.

Roll out dough on a floured surface so it forms a rectangle about 1/4" thick. In a small sauce pan over medium to low heat place the garlic cloves plus the butter melt the butter and cook the garlic until it is very soft. Brush with pastry brush the pizza dough with the melted butter and chop the soften garlic until it is minced and then spread out onto the dough; season the dough with garlic powder and Parmesan cheese. Spread the chopped broccoli evenly over the pizza dough and then spread the mozzarella and provolone cheese evenly also. Carefully roll the dough into a log by starting at one end and sealing edges with water and folding ends and tucking under log. Seam side on bottom of log. Carefully lift log onto cookie sheet pan and bake for about 30 to 45 minutes until golden brown and log sounds hollow and crisp.

Serve warm with a side of marinara sauce for dipping.

1/2 lb pizza dough (see recipe in the chapter entitled Everything Else)

16 oz chopped cooked broccoli

8 oz shredded mozzarella

8 oz shredded smoked provolone

1/4 Cup grated Parmesan cheese

1/4 Cup butter melted

4 crushed garlic cloves

2 Tbsp garlic powder

NOTES: *Broccoli cheese roll is an old favorite crowd pleaser that is good anytime. For a time saver purchase store bought pizza dough.*

STUFFED ZUCCHINI

24 Caps
Prep time: 25 minutes Total Time: 50 minutes

6 small zucchini ends cut off then cut about 24 caps 2" in length from each end and each end trimmed to set flat on surface until you have used all of the zucchini. Scoop out enough flesh of each cap with a melon ball scoop or teaspoon so the stuffing can fit inside of each cap.

In a large frying pan over medium heat, cook ground pork until brown with wooden spoon break up the ground meat to very small pieces. Add all ingredients except cheese, bread crumbs and parsley. Stir and breaking up any clumps into tiny pieces to incorporate; keep from burning until vegetables are soft, about 5 minutes. Now add the cheese, bread crumbs and parsley. Stir to incorporate and heat thoroughly about another minute.

Turn heat off and take off of stove. Stuff the hollow out caps with a teaspoon thoroughly with filling. Place caps in a greased glass baking pan in a preheated 350° F (175° C) oven for about 25-30 minutes until zucchini caps are soft and tender to the touch.

Tip: Grate the left over zucchini and use my Bolognese sauce (see recipe in the chapter entitled Everything Else) over top for another complete meal. I also use half lean ground veal and lean ground center cut pork for the meat.

NOTE: *These are great hors d'oeuvres at any party.*

1 1/2 lb ground pork

6 Tbsp olive oil

6 large white mushrooms minced

16 oz imitation crab meat broken into small pieces

2 tsp minced garlic

1/4 Cup minced onion

1 Cup unsalted butter

4 Tbsp Liquid Amino soy protein

2 Tbsp garlic powder

2 Tbsp onion powder

1 Cup Parmesan cheese

2 Cups multigrain bread crumbs

1/4 Cup fresh parsley chopped

SALMON PURSES

24 PURSES
Prep. Time: 15 minutes Total Time: 35 minutes

A delicious flaky, buttery crust filled with homemade basil pesto sauce and a piece of tender and flaky Atlantic salmon made into a purse for dipping into my homemade mustard dill sauce.

1 lb Atlantic salmon fillet cut into 1 inch cubes totaling 24 pieces

1 lb frozen puff pastry crust unrolled out on a flour surface (1 sheet cut into 12 rectangles and repeat for the other sheet)

1/2 Cup basil pesto sauce (see recipe in the chapter entitled Everything Else)

24 strings of green onions cut for ties

1 large egg beaten for wash

Preheat oven to 400° F (204° C).

On a well floured surface lay out one sheet of crust, cut 12 even rectangles and repeat for the other crust. Place about 1 tsp of pesto sauce in the middle of each rectangle and one cube of salmon on top. Dot each corner of each rectangle with a dab of water. Fold opposite corners together and fold and seal edges as well to form the purse. Take a string of onion and tie it around the neck of the purse and place on a lined cookie sheet leaving about 1 inch space between each purse. Repeat until all 24 purses have been made.

Brush with pastry brush the egg wash onto the purses. Place cookie sheet into the preheated oven for about 20 minutes until purses have a golden color.

Let cool and serve on a large platter with a side of mustard dill sauce for dipping.

TIP: Don't have pesto sauce made then just buy a good brand at your local supermarket.

Soup
&
Salads

Suzanne Schwendiman

CLAM CHOWDER SOUP

4-6 Servings
Prep time: 15 minutes Total time: 30 minutes

1 Cup celery thinly sliced
3 Tbsp butter
2 Tbsp flour
2 Cups seafood or Chicken broth
2 Cups peeled/diced russet potatoes
1 medium yellow onion chopped
2 1/2 Cups of whole white milk
4 slices bacon crisp cooked and crumbled
4 Cans of chopped clams with broth
Salt and Fresh Ground Pepper to taste

In a large saucepan cook celery and onions in butter over medium heat about 5 minutes or until tender. Stir in flour until combined. Stir in broth; bring to a boil, stirring constantly. Add potatoes and return to a boil. Reduce heat. Simmer uncovered for 15 minutes or until tender and potatoes are slightly mashed. Stir in milk, bacon and canned clams. Heat thoroughly. If desired thin with additional milk. Season the soup with salt and pepper to taste.

CHICKEN CHILI

4 Servings
Prep time: 15 minutes Total time: 30 minutes

1 medium yellow onion chopped

1 Tbsp olive oil

1 (15oz can) hominy, rinsed and drained

1 (15 oz can) great Northern beans rinsed and drained

1 (14 oz) chicken broth

9 oz of chopped chicken breast

1/4 Cup fresh lime juice

2 Tbsp chopped fresh cilantro

1/4 tsp ground cumin

1/4 tsp ground black pepper

1/2 Cup shredded Colby and Monterey Jack Cheese

1 (15 oz) bottle of green salsa

Tortilla chips and fresh chopped cilantro for garnishing

In a large saucepan cook onion in hot oil over medium heat for 3 minutes. Stir in hominy, beans, chicken broth, chicken, lime juice, cilantro, cumin and pepper. Cover and bring to boiling over high heat for about 15 minutes, stirring occasionally. Serve chicken chili in individual bowls then top each bowl with cheese, salsa, tortilla chips and fresh cilantro.

Suzanne Schwendiman

CORN CHOWDER

4 Servings
Prep time: 15 minutes Total time: 30 minutes

In a large saucepan cook celery, onion, red pepper and mushrooms in melted butter over medium heat for about 5 minutes or until tender. Sift in flour and stir until combined. Stir in broth, bring to a boil, stirring constantly. Add potatoes, return to a boil. Reduce heat, simmer uncovered for 15 minutes or until potatoes are tender/slightly mashed. Stir in milk, peas and corn. Heat thoroughly. If desired thin with additional milk. Season the chowder with black pepper and Chicken base to taste. Just before serving sprinkle crumbled bacon over each bowl.

NOTES: *If you desire, this chowder can be made with 1 or 2 chopped and cooked chicken breasts which really compliments the vegetables. Right before I serve the chowder I usually chop about 1 to 2 tsp of flat leaf parsley for a garnish for each bowl. If desire, substitute chicken broth for vegetable broth and chicken paste for vegetable bouillon cubes.*

1 Cup thinly sliced celery

1 medium yellow onion chopped

1 Cup diced red pepper

2 Cups fresh small white mushrooms cut in half

4 Tbsp butter

2 Tbsp flour

2 Cups of chicken broth

2 Cups peeled/diced russet potatoes

2 1/2 Cups of whole milk

4 slices crisp thick cut bacon crumbled

1 Cup petite frozen sweet peas

3 Cups fresh or frozen corn

Fresh ground black pepper to taste

2 Tbsp of Chicken bouillon base

Suzanne Schwendiman

GREENS AND BEANS SOUP WITH CHICKEN SAUSAGE

12 Servings
Prep time: 30 minutes Total time: 1 1/2 hours

The Chicken and Veal broth combination really gives this soup a unique flavor.

12 Cups Veal and Chicken Stock	2 lbs washed/drained and chopped collard greens
(See recipe in the chapter entitled Everything Else)	2 (15 oz can) navy beans drained (any kind on hand)
3 Tbsp olive oil	
3 Tbsp butter	2 (15 oz can) diced tomatoes or stewed
3 Cups diced carrots	1 lb rotisserie chicken pulled apart
3 Tbsp minced garlic	1 lb chicken sausage thinly diced (I used half chicken, tomato, mozzarella, garlic and half Chicken spinach, feta cheese combination)
3 Cups diced celery	
1 Cup diced onions	
1 Cup diced red/yellow peppers	3 to 4 Tbsp Chicken bouillon base
	2 Tbsp Beef bouillon base

In a large pot over medium to high heat melt the butter and oil together. Next add the diced carrots cook until slightly soft about 3 to 5 minutes. Add the remaining vegetables (garlic, celery, onions, and peppers). Cook covered until soft about 5 to 10 minutes. Take out vegetables and put in a food processor or blender to puree and set aside.

Pour broth into a large pot over medium/high heat add collard greens. Cook for about 30 minutes until greens are soft. Add chicken, sausage, beans and diced tomatoes cook for another 30 minutes. Add the chicken and beef paste stir until well incorporated. Add puree vegetables (will give broth a yellow color) and cook another 20 minutes until thoroughly heated through.

Serve in large bowls with a crusty loaf of bread.

TIPS: Make broth ahead of time to save time. Broth can be kept in refrigerator up to one week. Chicken sausage is similar to pork sausage links but instead of ground pork there is ground chicken mixed with seasonings, tomato, mozzarella or chicken mixed with spinach, feta cheese combination. The chicken sausage can be found in your local supermarket deli/meats section. Use any greens available to you or any you like examples spinach, leeks, bokchoy, cabbage, kale, Swiss chard, mustard greens etc.

Suzanne Schwendiman

COOL WATERMELON SOUP

6 Servings
Prep time: 10 minutes Total time: 1 hour

Served on a hot summer day will give you a "pick me up" for the rest of the day.

6 Cups seeded water melon cubes

1 pear peeled, cored/sliced

1 pint of fresh strawberries cleaned stems removed

1 tsp grated fresh ginger

1 Tbsp fresh lime juice

2 Tbsp honey

1/3 Cup thick plain yogurt or crème fresh (optional)

1 tsp chopped fresh mint (garnish optional)

In a food processor or blender add watermelon, pear, strawberries, ginger, lime juice and honey blend until smooth. Cover and chill for 1 hour.
Serve in chilled soup bowls and finish with a swirl of yogurt and mint.

NOTES: *I was inspired to make this when I was in New York City on a hot summer day and I had this as a special at a popular restaurant that day.*

WEDDING SOUP

4 – 6 Servings
Prep time: 15 minutes Total time: 30 minutes

A traditional soup that has an old world taste that warms the heart and the stomach.

8 Cups Veal Stock (see recipe in the chapter entitled Everything Else)

1 Cup carrot peeled and grated

16 oz chopped spinach frozen

1/2 Cup Orzo pasta or any very tiny pasta

12 oz rotisserie chicken pulled apart

20 veal/bison meatballs (recipe located in the chapter entitled "Meat & Poultry")

28 oz crushed tomatoes

28 oz fire roasted diced tomatoes

3 Tbsp Chicken Base

2 Tbsp Beef Base

Heat the broth in a medium soup pot over medium to low heat until boiling. Add in your meatballs, chicken spinach, carrots, crushed tomato and diced tomatoes. Cook for about 20 minutes. Just 10 minutes before serving add in the orzo pasta and the chicken and beef base. Cook until pasta has swollen in size and soft enough to eat.

Serve hot in soup bowls with the freshly grated parmesan cheese on top. On the side serve crusty bread.

NOTES: *Inspired from my growing up in an Italian neighborhood.*

CHEDDAR CHEESE BROCCOLI SOUP

6 – 8 Servings
Prep time: 15 minutes Total time: 30 minutes

A soup that has a creamy and cheesy broccoli taste that is great on its own or mixed in an omelet. The soup is quick and easy to make. It fills you up and warms the soul.

1 lb bag broccoli florets steamed	16 oz grated sharp cheddar cheese
1 Tbsp minced garlic	8 oz sour cream or plain yogurt
1 small yellow onion minced	6 Cups low sodium chicken broth
1 Tbsp olive oil	Salt & Pepper to taste
2 Tbsp unsalted butter	1/8 tsp turmeric
4 Tbsp flour	1 Tbsp chicken bouillon <u>base</u>

In a large pan over medium heat, add the oil and butter until melted. Add garlic and onion cook until soft about 3 minutes. Then sprinkle flour over the onion/garlic mixture, stir and cook for another minute until flour is cooked. Add chicken broth and broccoli. Stir and cook until broccoli is soft enough to be pureed. Add sour cream, with a hand held blender puree the soup so as to only see pieces of the broccoli floret. Add cheese and cook until melted and soup has thickened. Add chicken base, salt and pepper to taste, turmeric and stir completely to incorporate all the seasonings.

Serve hot in your favorite crusty bread bowls (use my nutty crunchy whole wheat baguette dough recipe to shape into small boule, let rise and bake until a golden color, cut a circle in top and take out stuffing enough for the soup to have room or mix into my omelet recipe).

NOTES: *This recipe was inspired because of my family's love for cheesy broccoli soup.*

Suzanne Schwendiman

POTATO LEEK SOUP

6 – 8 Servings
Prep time: 15 minutes Total time: 45 minutes

Delicious hearty soup with a creamy pale green broth that warms the soul.

2 Tbsp of olive oil	1/2 Cup of white wine or 2 tsp Dijon mustard
2 Tbsp minced fresh garlic	1 Tbsp dried crushed tarragon
3 large leeks sliced in thin circles and washed	1 Tbsp of dried crushed thyme
6 large russet potatoes diced (cooked in microwave)	1 Tbsp onion powder
1/2 lb bacon cooked/crumbled	1 Tbsp garlic powder
1 large carrot diced	1 Tbsp fresh ground black pepper
1/2 large onion chopped	2 Tbsp beef base
4 celery heart with leaves chopped	2 Tbsp chicken base
6 Cups chicken broth	2 Bay leaves
4 Cups water	25 oz plain fat free yogurt

Combine olive oil, garlic and leeks in a big pot on stove over medium heat cook until leeks are wilted. Add in potatoes, ¾ of bacon, carrot, onions, celery cook until wilted down. Then add you chicken broth, water, wine, seasonings (tarragon, thyme, onion and garlic powder and black pepper), beef and chicken base and bay leaves. Cook for about 20 -30 minutes until everything is soft.

Turn to low heat, take out bay leaves and use a hand held blender and blend until smooth, add the yogurt and blend again until smooth.

Serve in separate bowls with rest of bacon crumbled on top for garnish.

TIP: Just before putting tarragon and thyme into the soup, measure into the palm of your hand and then crush the herbs in your palm letting them fall into the soup so as to release the oils in these herbs.

24 HOUR VEGETABLE SALAD

10 Servings
Prep time: 20 minutes Total time: 24 hours

4 Cups torn crisp romaine lettuce	6 hard cooked eggs, sliced
4 Cups torn crisp red leaf lettuce	1 lb crisp cooked bacon crumbled
4 Cups torn crisp Boston or Bibb lettuce	10 oz frozen peas (<u>do not thaw</u>)
Salt, Black Pepper and Sugar to taste	1/2 Cup diced shallots
(about 1/2 tsp each per layer)	2 Cups real mayonnaise
2 Cups shredded mozzarella cheese	1/4 Cup thinly sliced green onions
2 Cups shredded Swiss cheese	

Place romaine in bottom of a large see through glass bowl. Sprinkle with salt, pepper, and sugar. Place red leaf lettuce on top and sprinkle again with salt, pepper and sugar. Mix the shredded cheeses together and use about half of cheese mixture for the next layer. Layer eggs a top of cheese and standing some slices on edge. Sprinkle generously with salt. Next layer in order half of the bacon, Boston or Bibb lettuce, peas and shallots. Spread mayonnaise heavily over top so as to seal and cover to edge of bowl. Cover with plastic wrap and chill 24 hours or overnight.

Serve chilled and garnish with remaining cheese, bacon and green onions before serving.

NOTES: *Inspired from an old recipe. There seems to be many versions of this salad but this is my family's favorite mixture.*

FRESH SEAFOOD SALAD

4 Servings
Prep time: 30 minutes Total time: 35 minutes

This trio combination of seafood is just right over a bed of fresh mixed greens.

Skewer the shrimp and scallops and season to taste with olive oil, salt, fresh ground black pepper and sweet smoked paprika. Place seasoned skewered shrimp and scallops on to a hot grill, turn temperature down to low and place seafood onto grill for about 2 – 4 minutes until the shrimp are pink and the scallops are no longer opaque yet firm to the touch. Squeeze lemon onto hot seafood.

Poach the chopped squid in boiling water with a half of lemon for about 5 minutes until firm and ends curl.

Toss all vegetables in salad bowl until combined evenly. Pour onto a large decorative plate; then arrange grilled and poached seafood on top. Sprinkle with crumbled goat cheese and serve slices of lemon on the side of plate as a garnish and also to be used for squeezing lemon onto salad. Drizzle with cold pressed extra virgin olive oil. Garnish with fresh chopped basil.

20 pieces of fresh blue shrimp	**10 chopped artichoke hearts**
10 pieces of fresh bay scallops	**1 large carrot shredded**
1/2 lb of fresh squid cleaned/chopped	**1/2 large purple onion thinly diced**
6 Cups mixed fresh greens	**1/2 large English cucumbers thinly diced**
10 chopped large pitted black olives	
2 large fire roasted grilled peppers	**1/4 Cup crumbled goat cheese**
	Salt, Fresh Ground Pepper, Sweet Smoked Paprika, squeezed lemon juice, olive oil, seasoning to taste

Served alongside of this is my tomato basil vinaigrette dressing (see recipe in the chapter entitled Everything Else). Also goes great with the whole wheat baguette recipe too (recipe under brunch & breads)

TIP: For a more luscious and filling salad serve your favorite fresh piece of grilled fish on top of salad too, season with olive oil, salt and pepper and sweet smoked paprika, plus fresh squeezed lemon after it comes off of grill. I suggest grouper, yellow fin tuna or Chilean sea bass. Also if you like add mussels and clams as well to the salad or any fresh combination of seafood available.

NOTES: *My friend and I loved this when we had something similar at a restaurant. I decided to make my own version so we could enjoy this recipe many times over.*

FRESH SUMMER SALAD

6-8 Servings
Prep time: 20 minutes Total time: 80 minutes

Such a refreshing taste on a hot summer day that leaves you feeling cooled and refreshed at the same time. It has a combination of lettuces, vegetables and fresh fruit that is in season. It can be served layered in a beautiful glass bowl. This salad pairs very nicely with a sweet citrus dressing.

3 Cups torn romaine lettuce	**2-3 fresh sweet peaches sliced**
3 Cups torn Bibb or Red Leaf lettuce	**1 pint of fresh strawberries sliced**
3 Cups baby leaf spinach	**3-4 kiwi peeled and sliced**
1 red bell pepper sliced	**2 oranges segmented**
1 green bell pepper sliced	**1 Cup fresh blueberries**
1 small fennel bulb sliced thinly	**16 oz grated sharp cheddar cheese**

Place about 3/4 of the torn romaine lettuce in a layered fashion in a large see through glass serving bowl. Next in a layered fashion scatter the sliced peaches evenly over the romaine lettuce. Next place the torn Bibb lettuce and the rest of the romaine lettuce in a layered fashion and some up the sides a little. Then layer the sliced strawberries on top of the lettuce. In a layered fashion spread out the spinach leaves. Next spread the remaining fruit in a mixed fashion plus fennel over the spinach. Top the fruit with cheese so that it is completely covered. Last layer is an alternative pattern in a circle fashion first slice of red pepper then green until you have covered the entire bowl with this pattern. Cover salad with plastic wrap and chill for at least 1 hour until ready to serve. Best made one day ahead of time so salad has longer time to chill in refrigerator.

Serve this beautiful arrangement of a salad with the citrus dressing (recipe under chapter entitled "Everything Else").

TIP: Use any combination of in season fresh fruit that day.

NOTES: *I made this salad for a hot 4th of July picnic and it was sensational.*

CREAMY SLAW SALAD WITH BLUE CHEESE

6 – 8 Servings
Prep time: 10 minutes Total time: 40 minutes

1/2 Cup shredded purple cabbage	3 Tbsp apple cider vinegar
1/2 Cup shredded radishes	3 Tbsp sugar
12oz package of broccoli slaw	2 Tbsp honey
14oz package of shredded cabbage	2 Tbsp black sesame seeds (<u>optional</u>)
1 1/2 Cup plain thick Greek yogurt (drained)	1/4 Cup crumbled blue cheese (<u>optional</u>)
1 dry package or 2 Tbsp of dried ranch dressing mix	

Thoroughly mix all ingredients into a large plastic bowl with a plastic or wooden spoon or spatula except for the cheese and sesame seeds. Place into refrigerator for at least 30 minutes. Just before serving stir thoroughly with wooden or plastic spoon again and garnish with cheese and sesame seeds.

NOTES: *This salad pairs wonderfully with the BBQ Tenderloin recipe, BBQ Pizza recipe and of course on top of hotdogs and hamburgers. The creaminess of this salad goes so well with the BBQ flavored recipes.*

Tip: Don't use a metal spoon; the live bacteria in yogurt will react to metal and can cause the bacteria to die.

Vegetables

WILTED SPINACH WITH LEEKS
&
PORTABELLA MUSHROOMS

4 Servings
Prep time: 10 minutes Total time: 20 minutes

3 large leeks diced washed thoroughly
1 lb fresh spinach washed and ready
2 tsp minced garlic
2 grilled portabella mushrooms minced
2 Tbsp olive oil
2 Tbsp Soy Protein (Liquid Amino)

Put 2 Tbsp of oil in a large skillet on medium heat along with garlic, cook until garlic is soft. Then add in the leeks and cook until bright green in color about 5-10 minutes. Then add the spinach, mushrooms and soy protein. Cook until most of the liquid has evaporated.

This is a nice complimentary side to my stuffed chicken recipe (under meat & poultry).

TIP: May use any greens in place of spinach.

Suzanne Schwendiman

SAUTÉ WINTER VEGETABLES

4 Servings
Prep time: 15 minutes Total time: 25 minutes

1/2 Cup sweet corn

1 medium turnip or rutabaga peeled cut into 1" cubes

3 carrots peeled and cut into 1" dice

1 parsnip peeled and cut 1" dice

1 yellow beet peeled and cut 1" dice

2 Jerusalem Artichokes (sunchokes) rubbed clean and cut 1" dice

1 Celery Root peeled and cut 1" dice

2 peeled butternut baby squash, cut into 1" cubes

3 Tbsp brown sugar

6 Tbsp unsalted butter

1 tsp ground cinnamon

1 tsp salt

2 tsp freshly ground black pepper

1 Tbsp of mint chopped

Blanch all the vegetables except the corn for 15-20 minutes until just before tender and cool in an ice water bath to retain bright color and stop cooking process quickly. Drain well.

Melt butter in a sauté pan over medium heat add sugar, cinnamon and stir until incorporated about 1 minute. Sauté all the vegetables including corn for 5 minutes or until softened and warmed thorough. Adjust seasoning with salt and black pepper. Serve warm on a large platter and garnish with mint.

NOTES: *These vegetables go so well with my pork chop recipe (under meat and poultry). Whatever root vegetables you find at your local market that day go well in this recipe.*

VEGETABLE MEDLEY CUP

6 Servings
Prep time: 20 minutes Total time: 30 minutes

In a large sauté pan cook 6 slices of bacon until crispy. Take out bacon, let cool then crumble, set aside for later. In the same sauté pan over medium heat add ginger, garlic, onions and all the spices (bouillon cube, curry, turmeric, cumin, cinnamon, salt and pepper). Sauté for about 5 minutes or until onions are light blond and soft, do not brown.

Add carrots, zucchini and cauliflower and sauté for about 10 minutes.

Add stock, stir and bring to a boil. Add frozen okra, stir, and cover and turn heat down to medium low to simmer for 10 minutes and then add frozen peas. Simmer for another 5 minutes or until all the vegetables are soft and most of liquid has evaporated. Toss in crumbled bacon, lime juice and chopped cilantro. Adjust seasoning with salt and pepper. Just before serving vegetable mixture in cups, swirl in yogurt and serve.

6 slices of thick cut bacon	1 Tbsp freshly grated ginger
1 large onion cut into 1/4" cubed slices	1 tsp minced garlic
	1 tsp curry powder
2 carrots peeled and diced	1 tsp turmeric powder
1 large zucchini or 2 small cut into 1/2" cubes	1 tsp cumin
	1 tsp cinnamon
1/4 lb cauliflower florets	3 Tbsp chopped cilantro
10 oz sliced frozen okra	salt & fresh ground black pepper to taste
10 oz petite peas frozen	
2 Cups vegetable stock or chicken	6 10" diameter soft tortilla shells
3 oz plain yogurt	place ramekins on tortilla shell & cut six 6" circles
1 vegetable bouillon cube	
1 lime juiced	six 4" sprayed with oil ramekins or 4" muffins pans

Preheat oven to 350° F (175° C).

Place each tortilla in 4" sprayed with oil ramekins or muffin pan and bake for 10-15 minutes or until lightly browned and set like a cup.

Serve vegetable medley in warm cups and garnish with a fresh cilantro leaf with stem on top of vegetable medley cup.

MINI LEANING TOWER OF EGGPLANT

6 Servings
Prep time: 20 minutes Total time: 40 minutes

This can be served as a great impressive appetizer or a main vegetarian dish along with steamed broccoli. It is even great served alongside any style of eggs.

Marinara Sauce:

2 Tbsp olive oil

1 onion diced

1 garlic clove minced

15 oz diced can tomatoes

1 tsp dried oregano

1 tsp dried basil

Salt & fresh ground black pepper to taste

Eggplants :

4 medium baby eggplants
(Japanese style if available, cut 1/2" slices 18 total)

salt & fresh ground pepper to taste

1 Cup flour

2 eggs beaten

1 1/2 Cup fresh bread crumbs

1/4 Cup parmesan cheese

1 Tbsp dried parsley

1 Cup oil for frying

4 tomatoes sliced 1/4"' thick (18 slices)

6 slices of mozzarella divided into 1/3's

6 slices of provolone divided into 1/3's

1/2 Cup balsamic vinegar reduced

Basil leaves for garnish

Preheat oven to 350° F (175° C).

MARINARA SAUCE: In a small saucepan over medium heat, warm oil and sauté onion for 1-2 minutes or until translucent. Add garlic and sauté, stirring continually. Do not brown. Add tomatoes and herbs and season with salt and pepper. Simmer for 10 minutes until most of liquid is gone. Set aside.

EGGPLANTS: Season eggplant slices with salt and pepper generously, and dredge in flour, shaking off the excess. Next dip each slice in egg, then into the bread crumb mixture (combine bread crumbs, parmesan cheese and dried parsley). Set aside on baking sheet lined with parchment paper. In large skillet heat oil over high heat until very hot. Sauté eggplant 4-5 slices at a time until golden brown on each side.

Place the cooked slices on a baking sheet, top each with a tomato slice and mozzarella and provolone cheese. Bake for about 15-18 minutes, until golden brown and cheese is melted.

BALSAMIC REDUCTION SAUCE: In a small saucepan, simmer vinegar until it's reduced by about 2/3's and reaches a syrup consistency. Set aside to cool.

To serve, stack three eggplant/tomato slices on each plate. Garnish with basil. Spoon marinara around eggplant tower and drizzle with Balsamic reduction sauce.

TIP: Sprinkle eggplants with salt and let them rest in a colander for an hour before preparing (known as degorging). Afterwards, rinse the slices under cold water. Gently squeezing out the moisture with a dry paper towel by pressing on the slices which also collapses the eggplant's air pockets so as to reduce the absorption of oil during frying. Helps rid eggplant of the bitter taste of alkaloid or if you can find a Japanese style eggplant it will not have that bitter taste. If you prefer you can use zucchini 1/4" cut slices instead of eggplant.

Suzanne Schwendiman

SAUTÉED RED CHARD WITH SMOKED TURKEY

4 Servings
Prep time: 15 minutes Total time: 30 minutes

It is a lovely combination of greens and smoked turkey that has a great taste without any need for seasoning.

2 Tbsp olive oil
1 small onion minced
3 garlic cloves minced
2 large bunch red chard washed and chopped
1 smoked turkey leg cooked and chopped
1 Cup chicken broth
1 vegetable bouillon cube

In a large frying pan over medium heat add oil, onions, garlic and cook until soft about 1 minute. Add your chopped Chard, diced smoked turkey leg, chicken broth and bouillon cube. Stir to incorporate all the ingredients. Continue cooking for about 15 minutes until chard is wilted and stir frequently until broth has completely evaporated.

Serve warm as a side dish or a main meal.

NOTES: *To spice this recipe up just add a few red peppers to the oil. Cannot find Red Chard, use kale , spinach, collard greens or mustard greens whatever is fresh and available at your local market.*

Suzanne Schwendiman

ROASTED SPAGHETTI SQUASH

4-6 Servings
Prep time: 5 minutes Total time: 1 hour

Squash that resembles spaghetti that has a roasted, buttery, cheese flavor and can be served by itself or with my homemade meat sauce.

Preheat oven to 350° F (175° C).

Place squash on a ungreased cookie sheet pan in oven for about 1 hour until squash shell is soft to touch and squash can be flaked with fork.

Take out of oven and scrape each squash shell with fork into a large heat resistance bowl until the squash is completely out of shell. Pour oil over the squash and continue to flake the squash with fork so as to mix in the oil. Sprinkle the cheese and garlic powder over the squash, mix and separate the squash with fork until all the oil, cheese and garlic powder are well incorporated.

1 large spaghetti squash cut in half
1/4 Cup parmesan cheese
1/4 Cup extra virgin olive oil
3 tsp garlic powder

Serve hot as a side dish or pour my homemade meat sauce on top of squash (recipe found under chapter entitled "Everything Else").

TIP: Put squash in microwave oven first for about 10-15 minutes then about 15-30 minutes in oven to speed up the cooking process.

Suzanne Schwendiman

ZUCCHINI LASAGNA

8 – 10 Servings
Prep time: 25 minutes Total time: 1 hour 30 minutes

A crisscross layered pattern of zucchini with my homemade beef sauce, rotisserie chicken, grilled portabella mushrooms and a white ricotta and mozzarella cheese sauce.

Preheat oven 375° F (190° C).

In hot boiling water blanch the zucchini strips for about 1 minute, drain and set aside.

In a mixing bowl combine pesto sauce, ricotta, sour cream, parmesan cheese, eggs and three cups bread crumbs, salt and pepper to taste until well combined.

In a 9 X 13" deep dish pan start with about a cup of homemade sauce spread thinly, then a layer of zucchini strips arranged perpendicular in an overlapping fashion (salt and pepper), next spread a thin layer of chicken (1 Cup), one whole mushroom, half of ricotta mixture and 1 cup grated mozzarella. The next layer of zucchini strips need to be layered horizontal in an overlapping fashion (salt & pepper), along with homemade meat sauce and ricotta mixture and mushroom. At the top end with overlapping perpendicular zucchini strips (salt & pepper), shredded mozzarella, fresh mozzarella and mix the remaining bread crumbs and 1/4 Cup of melted butter together; spread on top.

3 Cups homemade beef sauce (see recipe in the chapter entitled Everything Else)	2 Cups grated parmesan cheese
3-4 medium zucchini cut into 1/4" long slices	3 large eggs beaten
2 Cups shredded rotisserie chicken	4 Cups fresh bread crumbs
2 large grilled portabella mushrooms thinly sliced	2 Cups shredded mozzarella cheese
2 Cups basil pesto sauce (see recipe in the chapter entitled Everything Else)	16 oz fresh mozzarella 1/4" slices
	salt & pepper to taste
16 oz ricotta cheese	1/4 Cup melted butter
1/2 Cup sour cream	

Place 9 x 13" pan onto a cookie sheet pan with sides to help with spillage in oven for about an hour.

Take lasagna out of oven and let the lasagna rest for about 30 minutes or until set, cut and serve warm.

TIP: If you do not have beef sauce, rotisserie chicken and basil pesto sauce already prepared buy a good brand at your local market.

Pasta, Rice & Grains

Suzanne Schwendiman

QUINOA (KEEN-Wah)

4 Servings
Prep time: 5 minutes Total time: 10 minutes

You can add uncooked quinoa to soups or cooked to salads. You use it like you would rice or pasta. Quinoa is a grain and not pasta. Quinoa is an amino acid-rich (protein) seed which is gluten free and has a fluffy, creamy, slightly crunchy texture and a somewhat nutty flavor when cooked.

Bring the broth to a boil add the chicken base, quinoa and cook until the quinoa starts to look translucent. Do not overcook this should only take about 5-10 minutes. Keep covered and turn off the heat until liquid is absorbed completely. Fluff with fork and add the herbs. If you are familiar with cooking couscous then it is very similar.

Quinoa can be found in your local health food or local market stores throughout the year.

1 Cup of organic quinoa

2 Cups of chicken broth

1 Tbsp chicken bouillon base

2 Tbsp dry herbs or fresh herbs to water

TIP: The herbs I use are tarragon pairs nicely with chicken as the main course. I also use basil, thyme, parsley, cilantro, sage etc. depending on what is being served for the main course. To make completely vegetarian substitute the chicken broth and bouillon base for vegetable broth and vegetable bouillon cube.

BASIL PESTO RICE

4 Servings
Prep time: 5 minutes Total time: 25 minutes

Rice has never tasted so good with my fresh from the garden basil pesto sauce melted together to give it a delicious creamy, buttery flavor.

2 Cups cooked rice in chicken broth (brown or white)

2/3 Cup of basil pesto sauce (see recipe in the chapter entitled Everything Else)

Mix together the hot cooked rice with the pesto in a large bowl.

Serve hot with fish or a grilled steak.

GRILLED MUSHROOM & ASPARAGUS RISOTTO

4 – 6 Servings
Prep time: 15 minutes Total time: 30 minutes

*A fresh asparagus taste with grilled Portobello mushroom
in a creamy rice mixture that complement each other so nicely.*

1 large Portobello grilled and diced	4 1/2 Cups hot chicken broth
2 Tbsp minced garlic	1 Cup Arborio rice
1 small red onion minced	1 lb fresh diced asparagus
1 tsp dry tarragon crushed in palm	1/2 Cup grated parmesan cheese
1/8 tsp dry saffron crushed in palm/placed in broth (optional)	1/2 fresh lemon juiced
2 Tbsp extra virgin olive oil	salt & fresh ground pepper to taste
2 Tbsp butter	

Bring a quart of water in a sauce pan to a boil. Add a pinch of salt and lemon juice to water. Add the asparagus. Stir to incorporate ingredients for about 1-2 minutes until blanched, a little soft to the touch. At the end of 1-2 minutes, use a slotted spoon to remove the asparagus pieces to an ice water bath to shock the asparagus into a vibrant green color and to stop the cooking. Drain from the ice water bath and set aside.

In a 3 to 4 quart sauté pan, heat butter and oil on medium to high heat until butter is melted. Add the onions and garlic and cook for 1-2 minutes until translucent. Add the rice and cook for another 4 minutes more, stirring until nicely coated and the rice starts to brown slightly. Add 1/2 Cup of stock to the rice, plus 1 tsp of tarragon and stir gently until liquid is absorbed. Continue stirring and adding liquid until the liquid is almost completely absorbed, adding more stock in 1/2 Cup increments. Stir often to prevent the rice from sticking to the bottom of the pan. Continue cooking and stirring rice, adding a little bit of broth at a time (1/2 Cup), cooking and stirring until each 1/2 Cup increments are slowly absorbed, until the rice is very tender and creamy, about 20 to 25 minutes. Remove from heat.

Gently stir in the Parmesan cheese, the diced mushroom, and the asparagus. Add salt and pepper to taste.

TIP: Mix in 2 Tbsp of heavy cream for a richer taste and serve warm or add some grilled shrimp and scallops on top for a complete meal in one.

NOTES: *This recipe was inspired because of my family's love for risotto.*

BEEF CANNELLONI

6 – 8 Servings
Prep time: 25 minutes Total time: 45 minutes

Béchamel cheese sauce mixed with ground bison stuffed in a cannelloni shells and baked until a golden creamy color.

Bring a large (6-8 quarts) pot of lightly salted water to a boil. Add pasta and cook for 4 minutes. Drain and set aside. Do not overcook pasta. It only needs to start the cooking process so noodle should be soft to touch but firm enough to stuff.

Preheat oven to 350° F (175° C).

In a large skillet on medium heat sauté oil, half of onion and half of garlic until soft about 1-2 minutes. Add ground meat, salt and black pepper to taste, thyme and oregano cook until meat is browned (about 5-10 minutes). Break up meat into very tiny pieces with the back of wooden spoon.

In the meantime over low to medium heat in a medium heavy sauce pan, melt butter until it starts to foam, add the flour, and mix well with a wooden

1 (8oz) package cannelloni or manicotti pasta	2 tsp fresh ground black pepper
1 lb ground bison or fresh ground steak	1/4 Cup unsalted butter
1 medium yellow onion minced	1/4 Cup flour
6 cloves garlic minced	2 1/2 Cups milk
3 Tbsp olive oil	16 oz grated or cubed Fontana cheese
1 Tbsp dried thyme crushed in palm	1/4 Cup grated Parmesan cheese
1 Tbsp dried oregano crushed in palm	1/2 tsp white pepper
2 tsp salt	1/8 tsp fresh ground nutmeg

spoon. Cook over low heat 1-2 minutes, stirring constantly to incorporate and cook flour. Remove pan from heat and let stand, up to 10 minutes. In another medium sauce pan over medium heat for about 3-4 minutes, scald milk (heating it until just below boiling point). Return saucepan with roux to medium to low heat. Add all of the milk at once (to avoid the formation of lumps). Simmer, stirring gently with a wire whisk, add rest of onion, garlic, all of the cheese, white pepper and nutmeg, whisking until velvety smooth and thick (15-20 minutes).

Mix about half white sauce with meat mixture and stuff each cannelloni with about 3 tablespoons of mixture. Don't be afraid to stuff the cannelloni by using your clean hands. Place stuffed cannelloni in a 9 x 13" glass greased baking pan. Cover top of stuffed cannelloni with rest of white sauce and bake in the oven for about 20 minutes or until sauce is bubbly.

BAKED ZITI

6 – 8 Servings
Prep time: 20 minutes Total time: 1 hour

This recipe is so incredibly easy and a delicious baked pasta.

1 lb ziti cooked and drained

32 oz whole milk ricotta

6-8 Cups Marinara Sauce (recipe is located in the recipe entitled <u>Meatballs in Marinara Sauce</u> under chapter entitled "Meat & Poultry") or you may use the Bolognese Sauce located in the chapter entitled "Everything Else"

16 oz grated mozzarella

Preheat oven to 350° F (175° C).

Drain your hot pasta and place in a large deep dish baking pan. Add your sauce and ricotta and stir until the ingredients are well incorporated. Add the grated mozzarella on top and put into a preheated 350° F oven for about 45-60 minutes until top is slightly browned and cheese is melted.

NOTES: *I served this to my family while on vacation and it was such a sensational dish.*

HOMEMADE PESTO PASTA

1 1/2 LB PASTA DOUGH
Prep time: 25 minutes Total time: 1 1/2 hours

Pesto adds a beautiful color and delicious flavor to homemade pasta.

8 oz Basil Pesto sauce (see recipe in the chapter entitled Everything Else)	6 Quarts Boiling Water
1 Tbsp water	2 tsp salt
4 large eggs	1 Tbsp oil
4 Cups sifted unbleached all purpose flour or substitute	
1 Cup for wheat flour	

Using the bowl to your mixer place pesto, water eggs and flour in the bowl, attach bowl and flat beater. Turn to speed 2 for 30 seconds. Exchange flat beater for dough hook. Turn to speed 2 and knead 2 minutes. Remove dough from bowl and hand knead for 1-2 minutes. Divide dough into eight pieces keep in plastic bag until ready to be used so as not to dry out the dough before processing with Pasta Sheet Roller attachment. Follow instructions to fettuccini, spaghetti, and angel hair or pasta sheet roller for lasagna and ravioli for the pasta cutter attachments.

Instead of pasta roller attachments roll one part at a time into paper thin rectangles on generously floured surface with rolling pin (keep remaining dough covered with a moist towel so not to dry out). Loosely fold rectangle lengthwise into thirds; cut crosswise into 1/4" strips. Unfold floured strips and place on towel to dry or drying rack for up to 1 hour.

Shaping pasta an example of this could be orrchietta (Puglia's little ear shaped pasta) by taking a piece of dough and rolling into a 1" diameter and 12" long log. Using a butter knife cut 1/2" section off of log until it is all into 1/2" pieces then using the knife curl each 1/2" piece like you would butter. Using your thumb and forefinger having the curl side facing you put the dough onto thumb and roll the dough with forefinger. It should resemble a hat, let dry for about 4-5 hours.

Add salt and oil to boiling water. Gradually add pasta and continue to cook at a boil until pasta is al dente or slightly firm to the bite (2-5 minutes depending on thickness of pasta). Pasta floats to the top of the water while cooking, so stir occasionally to keep it cooking evenly. Drain in a colander.

TIP: Serve with my favorite meat sauce (see recipe in the chapter entitled Everything Else) or toss with heated extra virgin olive oil with crushed roasted garlic and Parmesan cheese or to spice it up add a few red peppers to the oil.

NOTES: *This recipe was inspired when my husband was enjoying a pasta dish at one of our favorite restaurants.*

Fish
&
Seafood

Suzanne Schwendiman

CHILEAN SEA BASS WITH ORANGE SAUCE

4 Servings
Prep time: 15 minutes Total time: 20 minutes

Thick, white, flaky cut of fish served over a bed of wilted spinach
with a sweet orange sauce drizzled on top for flavor and color.

On stove top with a large pan with water enough to cover fillets, place lemon and juice plus ginger into hot boiling water. Place fillets into water and cook until fillets flake about 5-8 minutes depending on thickness.

Meanwhile in a large sauce pan filled with boiling water, place spinach in water, cook until wilted about 30 seconds and drain well, place a cup of wilted spinach on each plate. In another small sauce pan on medium heat add orange juice plus zest, cream, jello mix and cayenne pepper stir until jello mix is dissolved and sauce is very warm (too thick add hot water to thin so as to drizzle over fillets). Take out fillets and let drain a few seconds and place fillets over hot spinach. Drizzle warm orange glaze sauce over fillets more or less depending on how sweet you like your dish. Serve immediately.

4 Chilean Sea Bass fillets thick cut 4 oz
1 lb (454 grams) baby spinach washed/drained
1 lemon juiced
3 slices of fresh ginger (1/4" thick)

Orange Sauce:
4 oz dry orange jello mix
1 orange juiced with zest
1/2 Cup heavy cream
1/8 tsp cayenne pepper

NOTES: *Quick, delicious, healthy and most of all, easy for a fabulous dinner or party.*

FILLET OF COD WITH A PESTO CRUST

4 Servings
Prep time: 15 minutes Total time: 30 minutes

4 (6oz) fillet of cod (or any white fresh meaty fish)

1/2 lb or 2 stick of butter, room temperature

2 Tbsp margarine

1/2Cup basil pesto sauce (see recipe in the chapter entitled Everything Else)

3 Tbsp fresh minced chives

3 large eggs

2 Cups freshly ground white bread crumbs

salt & freshly ground black pepper to taste

Preheat oven to 350° F (175° C).

For crust, in a large mixing bowl, whip butter and margarine with an electric mixer, at medium to high speed until doubled in size. Add pesto sauce, chives and mix well. Add eggs bread crumbs and adjust seasoning with salt and pepper about 1 tsp each. Whip for 2 minutes and set aside.

Arrange fillets on a baking pan, pat dry, and season with salt and pepper. Place crust mixture on top, level off to 1/4" thick. Bake for 12-15 minutes until fish is flaky and crust is golden.

TIP: Serve on top of mashed potatoes with a side of sautéed vegetables.

ALASKAN HALIBUT WITH A COMPOTE SAUCE

4-6 Servings
Prep time: 15 minutes Total time: 80 minutes

Sautéed halibut with a vegetable Compote sauce which is poured over the top and gives this fish an herbal flavor that leaves you wanting more.

On top of the stove over medium heat in a large frying pan sauté first six ingredients for about 5-10 minutes or until all ingredients are soft. Add your crushed tomatoes stir periodically to incorporate the ingredients and cook for about 1 hour until sauce has thickened. Season sauce with oregano, thyme, parsley by crushing the ingredients into palm of hand until they are more like a powder. Add garlic and onion powder, salt and pepper, vegetable cubes, and the wine. Stir all the ingredients until the ingredients are well incorporated. With handheld blender or food processor puree the sauce until all the ingredients are well incorporated about 1-2 minutes. Keep sauce on a low flame with a tilted cover until fish is cooked.

Meanwhile rub the fish with the remaining oil and old bay seasoning and salt and pepper. In a large greased frying pan over medium to high heat sauté fish on skin side down for about 2-5 minutes, add butter and carefully flip the fish over for another 2-5 minutes or until fish flakes.

Serve fish warm on a large platter with Compote sauce poured on top generously. On top of that sprinkle the cheese, add the tapenade on top with lemon zest and squeeze lemon juice plus drizzle extra virgin olive oil over entire platter.

TIP: Serve warm over your favorite pasta or over a garden salad, the warm and cold salad complement each other very nicely. Or you may use my baguette recipe found under the bread section and cut the warm bread length wise and serve over the top of the bread.

Sauce Ingredients:

2 Tbsp minced garlic

1 small red onion minced

1 fennel bulb chopped

1 carrot chopped

4 celery stalks diced

4 Tbsp extra virgin olive oil

28 oz can crushed tomatoes

2 tsp dry oregano crushed in palm

2 tsp dry thyme crushed in palm

1 Tbsp dry parsley crushed in palm

1/2 Cup red table wine or vegetable stock

2 tsp garlic powder

2 tsp onion powder

1 tsp fresh ground black pepper

1 tsp salt

2 vegetable bouillon cubes

Fish Ingredients:

2 Tbsp extra virgin olive oil

4-6 (4oz) fillets of halibut or any white

Meaty fish that is fresh that day

2 tsp old bay seasoning

1/2 tsp salt

1/2 tsp freshly ground black pepper

2 Tbsp unsalted butter

Garnish Ingredients:

1/4 Cup freshly grated Parmesan Cheese

1 lemon zest plus juice

2 Tbsp olive tapenade (minced black olives)

2 Tbsp Extra Virgin Olive Oil

Suzanne Schwendiman

PUFF PASTRY WRAPPED SALMON

4 Servings
Prep time: 20 minutes Total time: 45 minutes

*A delicious flaky, buttery crust filled with my homemade basil pesto sauce
and a piece of tender and flaky Atlantic salmon.*

4 (4oz) Atlantic salmon fillets

1 lb frozen puff pastry crust

1/4 Cup basil pesto sauce (see recipe in the chapter entitled Everything Else)

Slices of lemon for garnish

8 springs of dill for garnish

1 large egg for wash

Preheat oven to 400° F (204° C).

On a well floured surface lay out a piece of crust large enough to cover the fillet like a package. Place a fillet in middle of each pastry piece and pour 2-3 Tbsp of pesto sauce in middle. Fold salmon like a package into 1/3 and tuck ends underneath. Repeat until all fillet and pesto sauce are wrapped with puff pastry. Beat egg and brush crust with pastry brush the egg wash onto the outside of crust.

Place on a greased cookie sheet in oven for about 20-25 minutes until pastry is golden brown.

Take out place on platter garnish with lemon slice and dill spring.

TIP: Serve with a side of my homemade cucumber dill sauce (see recipe in the chapter entitled Everything Else) for dipping.

PARMESAN DILL CRUSTED BAKED STEELHEAD TROUT

4 Servings
Prep time: 5 minutes Total time: 45 minutes

A delicious white parmesan cheese and dill sauce baked on top to form a golden crust over a fresh piece of Steelhead Trout.

1 lb Steelhead Trout (deboned/cleaned)

1 Cup mustard dill sauce (see recipe in the chapter entitled Everything Else)

1/3 Cup freshly grated Parmesan cheese

Preheat oven to 300° F (148° C)

Place trout in a 9 x 13" greased glass pan topped by spreading dill sauce over trout and generously sprinkling cheese on top.

Bake in oven for about 25-35 minutes until trout flakes.

TIP: Serve this recipe with my quinoa recipe (located in the chapter section entitled "Pasta, Rice and Grains").

NOTES: *This recipe was inspired for the need of more delicious and healthy recipes. Steelhead Trout is a farmed raised salmon that is milder in taste but has a bright red color to the flesh; this is how you know it is fresh.*

Suzanne Schwendiman

CITRUS BAKED TILAPIA

4 Servings
Prep time: 5 minutes Total time: 20 minutes

Low and slow cooking method allows the oils to melt into this fish to flavor it
so it will have a moist, soft, tender and delicious taste of Tilapia with a hit of lemon spice seasoning.
This recipe goes great with any grilled or steamed vegetables.

1 lb fresh Tilapia (deboned/cleaned)
2 Tbsp olive oil
2 Tbsp Citrus Seasoning (dry ground spices i.e. salt, sugar red pepper, garlic onion, lemon peel, paprika)

Preheat oven 300° F (148° C)

Rub 1 tablespoon of olive oil on each side of the Tilapia and then rub 1 tablespoon of citrus seasoning on each side of Tilapia place in a clear glass baking dish in a preheated oven until fish flakes about 15 minutes.

TIP: Using another fish that is oily, do not rub oil on to fish, just the citrus seasoning. Also you may wrap fish into a parchment package. Adjust the cooking time for more if fish is thicker.

NOTES: *A Fish lover's recipe.*

Meat
&
Poultry

Suzanne Schwendiman

PIZZA ON THE GRILL

One 12" x 24" pizza
Prep time: 10 minutes Total time: 15 minutes

A thin crispy and crunchy crust with a Smokey grilled flavor. Topped with a parsley pesto sauce and smoked provolone cheese, purple onions and delicious, moist barbecue smoked chicken.

1/4 - 1/2 lb Wheat Dough (see recipe in the chapter entitled Everything Else)

1 Cup Parsley pesto sauce (see recipe in the chapter entitled Everything Else)

2-3 Cups shredded smoked provolone

1/4 Cup thinly sliced purple onions

2-3 Cups rotisserie chicken

1 Cup of finishing BBQ Sauce (see recipe in the chapter entitled Everything Else)

1/4 Cup course ground yellow corn

1/2 Cup all purpose flour

Preheat outside grill to 500° F – 600° F (260° C).

In a medium bowl mix the **BBQ Sauce** and chicken together so as to saturate the chicken entirely and set aside.

Roll room temperature dough onto a well floured surface about 2mm thick 12" x 24" in diameter. Generously spread ground corn onto your wooden pizza peel. Fold dough into thirds, by using dough cutter/dough scraper, pushing flour dust under crust to gently pick up the dough to transfer to peel.

Turn grill to low and take peel with dough and slide the pizza on to hot grill, cover for about 1-2 minutes until bubbles start to form on crust. Generously spread right to the edge of pizza with parsley pesto sauce. Next spread evenly the grated provolone, onions and barbecue chicken on to pizza. Turn grill back to medium and cover and cook another 2-3 minutes until pizza is bubbling hot. Use metal peel to slide dough around to get grill marks on bottom evenly.

Remove pizza from grill and place on a well floured or ground corn surface and let rest for 1-2 minutes and cut and serve.

NOTES: *This can be turned into a complete meal by serving with my slaw salad with blue cheese. For a quick version buy premade dough roll out and put on grill with your favorite toppings.*

STUFFED GRILLED PORK CHOPS WITH PEACH MARMALADE SAUCE

6 Servings
Prep time: 15 minutes Total time: 20 minutes

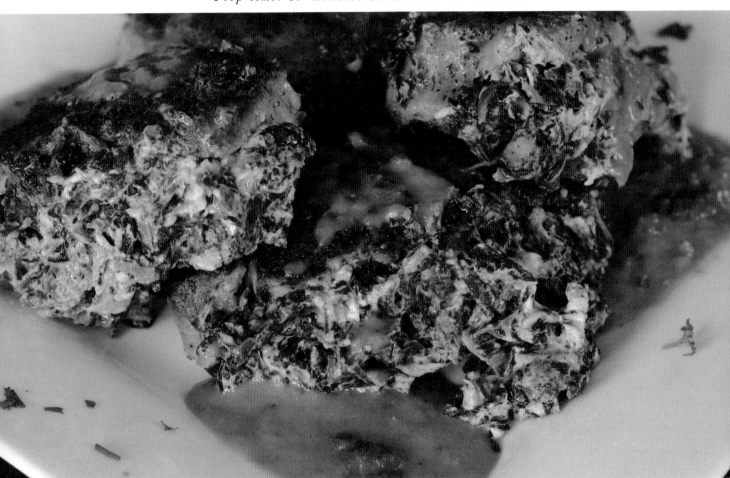

Sweet and savory taste of a thick center cut pork chop stuffed with spinach, crumbled blue cheese, cream cheese and sun dried tomatoes that will make you a lover of chops again.

6 (6oz) thick center-cut pork chops

2 Tbsp olive oil

2 cloves garlic minced

6 sun-dried tomatoes, diced thinly

1 (10oz) bag of frozen spinach (thawed, excess water removed)

1/2 tsp dried thyme crushed in palm

1/4 Cup crumbled blue or feta cheese (2 oz)

1/2 Cup cream cheese (4oz)

1 Cup chicken broth

1/2 lemon zest plus juiced

2 Tbsp Dijon Mustard

1/2 Cup Peach Marmalade (see recipe in the chapter entitled Everything Else)

Salt & Freshly Ground Black Pepper

In a medium sauté pan over medium heat add the one tablespoon of oil, garlic and cook until soft about 1 minute. Add the tomatoes, spinach, thyme salt and pepper to taste, cook and stir to combine about 2 minutes. Transfer mixture to a bowl, add the cheese by stirring to combine completely; set aside.

Using a sharp knife cut a pocket into the thickest portion of the pork chop so about 1/4 of the spinach mixture can fit into pork chop. Stuff each pocket with the spinach mixture and close the pork around the stuffing (stuffing will be bulging out). Season the outside of the pork chops with salt and pepper.

In a small bowl whisk the chicken broth, lemon zest plus juice, mustard and peach marmalade together and set aside.

In the same sauté pan as the spinach mixture was cooked in over medium to high heat add the remaining oil and heat pan to hot. When the pan is hot add the stuffed seasoned pork chops to pan, cover and sear on both sides for about 4 minutes per side until the juices run clear. Transfer the pork to a serving platter and tent with foil to keep warm. Now add the chicken broth mixture to the same pan over medium to high heat simmer and reduce broth by half by stirring the sauce so as to make a light sauce about 8 minutes.

Serving Suggestion: Serve the pork chop on top of warm garlic/parmesan mashed cauliflower with a side of vegetables and garnish with rosemary spring.

SALT & PEPPER PORK CHOPS

4 Servings
Prep time: 5 minutes Total time: 10 minutes

Pork Chops that are so delicious to the taste that it leaves you wanting more every time.

4 thin cut pork chops (1/2" thick)
4 pieces of thick cut hickory smoked bacon (using fat from bacon to fry pork chops)
Salt & fresh ground black pepper to taste

Fry bacon in a large cast iron pan until crispy. Take bacon out of pan and place on paper towel to cool and drain (maybe used over cooked green beans). Salt and pepper the pork chops. Place pork chops in the same pan on high heat so as to have pan very hot before chops are put in pan. Cook the chops for 1 minute and then turn over to cook another minute on the other side until firm to touch (internal temp 170° F or 75° C).

Serving Suggestion: Serve hot with mash potatoes and gravy with cut green beans and crumbled bacon on top.

MEATBALLS IN MARINARA SAUCE

6-8 Servings
Prep time: 20 minutes Total time: 30 minutes

The fresh ground veal and ground bison meat mixture is what gives these meatballs a real homemade taste that will have you coming back for more.

MEATBALL PREPARATION: Mix all meatball ingredients together until well incorporated no longer than 1-2 minutes with your clean hands. In a large sauté pan over medium heat with about 3-4 Tbsp of olive oil heated form small meatballs about 2 inches in diameter and put them in the pan to sauté. When completed forming meatballs and putting them into oil turn them over to sauté on other side for about another 2-5 minutes until juices are clear and meatball no longer has soft center.

MARINARA SAUCE PREPARATION: In a large mixing bowl put all sauce ingredients into bowl and blend with hand held blender until well incorporated about 2 minutes or pour into a blender and pulse until well incorporated.

Pour sauce over sautéed meatballs and simmer covered for about 10 minutes.

Serve over penne pasta or in a sub roll for meatball subs.

Meatballs:
(about 60 small meatballs)

1 lb ground bison or ground sirloin

1 lb fresh ground veal

2 large eggs beaten

1 1/2 Cups freshly ground multigrain bread crumbs

2 Tbsp minced garlic

3 Tbsp dried parsley or fresh chopped parsley

2 Tbsp dried oregano

1 Cup freshly grated Parmesan cheese

2 tsp freshly ground pepper

4 Tbsp Liquid Amino

4 Tbsp olive oil plus more for frying

Marinara Sauce:

2 (28 oz) whole peeled tomatoes

2 oz tomato paste

1 Tbsp dried oregano or marjoram

1 Tbsp dried parsley

1 Tbsp onion powder

1 Tbsp garlic powder

½ BEEF & ½ TURKEY LOAF

2 POUNDS
Prep Time: 20 Total Time: 1 1/2 hours

A meat lover's paradise, one side is moist, delicious, and tender beef. The other side is moist, delicious, and savory turkey for a healthy meal. The meatloaf is cooked in a bread machine that cooks it on a very low temperature to seal in all of the juices that are delicious to the taste. Picture shown with Finishing BBQ Sauce.

1 lb fresh chopped steak	1 lb fresh ground lean turkey
1 packet of beefy onion soup mix	1 medium yellow onion minced
1/4 Cup water	4 garlic cloves minced
1 medium yellow onion minced	1/2 Cup fresh herbs minced together (sage, cilantro, parsley)
2 large eggs beaten	1/2 Cup freshly grated Parmesan cheese
1 1/2 Cups wheat bread crumbs	
1/2 Cup Grated Parmesan Cheese	1 Tbsp gourmet burger seasoning (i.e. salt, onion, tomato, red/green bell pepper, smoked flavoring and molasses)
1 Tbsp soy protein (liquid amino)	
1 Tbsp Worcestershire sauce	
2 tsp onion powder	1 tsp poultry seasoning
2 tsp garlic powder	2 tsp garlic powder
1 tsp freshly ground black pepper	2 tsp onion powder
4 garlic cloves minced	1 1/2 Cups wheat bread crumbs
1/4 Cup fresh herbs cilantro/parsley mix	2 large eggs beaten
2 Tbsp extra virgin olive oil	2 Tbsp Soy Protein (Liquid Amino)
	4 Tbsp grape seed oil or extra virgin olive oil

In a separate bowl combine all first 15 ingredients until well incorporated using your clean hands about 1-2 minutes.

Place the beef mixture in one end of bread machine pan (2 lb loaf size).

In a second bowl combine the remaining ingredients for the turkey mixture until well incorporated using your clean hands about 1-2 minutes.

Place the turkey mixture in the other end of bread machine pan so as to seal the two ends together. Select only the baking method and cook for 70 minutes or internal temperature reaches 170° F or 75° C.

An alternative method can be using a 2lb glass bread pan (10.5 x 5.5 x 12") in a preheated 300° F or 150° C for about 4 hours or until internal temperature reaches 170° F or 75° C. Before placing the loaf into oven wrap the entire pan with aluminum foil to seal in the juices.

OPTIONAL TIP: If you desire, prior to 30 minutes at the end of baking time pour on top of loaf a glaze and let the glaze caramelize on top.

Another alternative to the glaze recipe, I use my favorite barbecue sauce instead of the glaze sauce (recipe located in section "Everything Else")

GLAZE SAUCE:

1/2 Cup ketchup

1 Tbsp brown sugar

1 tsp of prepared mustard

Suzanne Schwendiman

PUFF PASTRY WRAPPED FILET MIGNON

6 Servings
Prep time: 10 Total time: 40 minutes

Nothing is better than a delicious flaky, buttery crust with mushroom pesto sauce, provolone cheese and a juicy and delicious portion of filet mignon, wrapped together in a beautiful puff pastry package.

6 (4oz) fillet mignon seasoned with olive oil and salt/pepper, seared on a hot grill about 1 minute per side

1 lb frozen puff pastry crust

6 slices provolone cheese

3/4 Cup mushroom pesto sauce (see recipe in the chapter entitled Everything Else)

1 egg beaten for wash on crust

Preheat oven to 400° F (205° C).

On a well floured surface lay out a piece of puff pastry enough to cover the fillet like a package. Place a fillet in middle of each pastry piece and pour 2-3 Tbsp of mushroom pesto sauce in middle, top with a slice of cheese. Fold fillet like a package into thirds and tuck ends underneath. Repeat until all fillets, pesto sauce and cheese are wrapped with puff pastry. Beat egg and brush crust with pastry brush with the egg wash.

Place on a greased cookie sheet in oven for about 25-30 minutes until pastry is golden brown.

Take out place on a serving platter garnish with a dollop of your favorite sour cream and chives.

TIP: If you desire your fillet to be well done cook about 2-3 minutes longer per side on the hot grill.

CROCK POT SMOKED PORK TENDERLOIN

6-8 Servings
Prep time: 15 minutes Total time: 8-10 hours

Juicy, tender, hickory smoked pork tenderloin that is just so moist; it falls apart without any work.

1 large Crock Pot	8 oz of liquid hickory smoke
1 large hickory smoker aluminum bag	2 Tbsp garlic powder
(can be found online)	2 Tbsp onion powder
2 lbs pork tenderloin	1 Tbsp sweet smoked paprika
1 whole floret of garlic crushed	
2 large onions sliced	

Put Crock Pot on low for about 8 or 10 hours. In a separate small bowl combine by stirring the garlic, onion and paprika powders, then rub the tenderloin with the garlic, onion, and paprika mixture. Place the coated tenderloin into a smoker bag along with the crushed garlic cloves, onion slices and liquid smoke. Seal bag and place into Crockpot on low for about 8-10 hours.

When Crock Pot is done take out and separate meat from onion slices and garlic serve with my homemade barbecue sauce (recipe located in the chapter entitled "Everything Else").

SERVING SUGGESTIONS: Goes very well with my homemade slaw recipe (recipe located in the chapter entitled "Soup & Salads" section).

NOTES: *This recipe is so easy that you will not miss those long hours of cooking with your smoker.*

Tip: If you do not have a Crockpot put on a baking sheet into a preheated 275° F or 135° C oven for about 4-5 hours until internal temperature reaches 150° F (65° C).

STUFFED CHICKEN BREAST

6 Servings
Prep time: 15 minutes Total time: 25 hours

*Very unique and versatile, because of the way it can be prepared, a few different ways to get different tastes,
depending on what flavor you are most interested in. Stuffed Chicken breast is a crowd pleaser.*

6 large boneless skinless chicken breasts

4 1/2 Cup real mayonnaise

1/4 to 1/2 Cup Red Hot Chili Sauce (Thai) depending if you want it spicy

OPTIONAL DRY RUB: OR see Meat Marinade Recipe found under section called Everything Else

1 tsp curry powder	**1 tsp mace powder**
1 tsp turmeric powder	**1 tsp poultry seasoning**
1 tsp chili powder	**1 tsp cumin powder**
1tsp garlic powder	**1 tsp celery powder**
1 tsp onion powder	**1 tsp black pepper**

2 lemons juiced or limes put whole lemons or limes into marinade

STUFFING INGREDIENTS:

Grilled portabella mushroom

3 slices provolone cheese

3 slices prosciutto

See Meat Marinade recipe in the chapter entitled Everything Else section. Place chicken in freezer gallon zip lock bag with whatever dry powders you like to rub your chicken in or have handy. You can even skip the rub step and just add in a Thai spicy Chili sauce instead of the rub then the mayonnaise, massage the meat for about 1-2 minutes until all pieces have been thoroughly coated. Keep chicken marinade in refrigerator for up to 24-48 hours, massage meat everyday for 1-2 minutes. Add fresh cut squeezed limes or lemons to the marinade. You can alter the seasoning to acquire your best flavor savory, sweet or spicy.

After the meat has marinade for sufficient enough time then grill the chicken on a hot outdoor grill (650° F or 343° C), turn flame to low when placing chicken onto grill, cook until temperature just before it reaches 170° F or 75° C until chicken is firm but do not overcook, turn chicken over half way through cooking process (instead of grilling chicken you can coat chicken with bread crumbs and fry in fryer or bake in oven until internal temp reaches 170° F (75° C).

You can use the chicken as a main meal as is, cut up, put on salad, or make sandwiches with the breast. I split the breast open and put in a few slices of grilled portabella mushroom, 1/2 slice of provolone cheese, 1/2 slice of prosciutto and heat through in 350° F (175° C) oven until cheese is melted about 10-15 minutes.

SUZANNE'S CHICKEN

6 Servings
Prep time: 30 minutes Total time: 25 hours

The way chicken was intended to be served. Fire roasted chicken breast topped with sautéed spinach, grilled artichokes, Chevre goat cheese, and with a drizzle of lemon basil sauce.

6 large boneless skinless chicken breast (marinaded in Meat Marinade recipe under Everything Else section using only the Thai/mayo option)

1 lb (454 grams) baby spinach washed drained

12 artichoke hearts cut in half (packaged in water)

6 (1" thick slices) Chevre goat cheese

1 stick unsalted butter (115 grams)

1/4 Cup minced fresh basil

2 lemons juiced with zest

After sufficient time has passed for marinating the meat place chicken on a hot 650° F (343° C) outdoors grill, turn flame to low before placing chicken on grill. Cook chicken just before internal temperature reaches 170° F (75° C), should be slightly firm to the touch and the chicken will be blacken, turn chicken over half way through the cooking process. Might need to spritz grill with water to keep flames from engulfing chicken. Place artichokes on hot grill to have grill marks. On the stove (medium heat) in oiled pan place spinach, cook just before wilted. Take out and place on top of warm grilled chicken. On top of spinach place the two grilled artichokes on each piece of chicken. Then place the goat cheese slice on each breast. In a small sauce pan on medium heat melt butter add lemon juice with zest and basil stir and take off of stove and drizzle over chicken breast. Add more sauce over chicken if you desire.

NOTES: *This recipe was inspired from eating at one of my favorite restaurants.*

Desserts

MOIST CHOCOLATE RED VELVET CAKE

3 (9 1/2 "Round Cake Pans)
Prep time: 20 minutes Total Time: 1 hour 20 minutes

Rich red velvet cake that is so moist with a chocolate taste that never disappoints the taste buds.
It is so delicious that it can be eaten without any frosting.
This recipe has a bonus recipe that makes great gifts; they are out of this world Red Velvet White Coconut Truffles.

Main Ingredients:

3 (9 1/2" round cake pans) lightly spray with oil

3 1/2 Cups all purpose white flour sifted

3 Cups granulated white sugar

3 tsp baking soda

2 tsp salt

1/2 Cup Dutch Processed Dark Cocoa

2 Cups Extra Virgin Coconut Oil room temperature

2 Tbsp white vinegar + milk to equal 1 Cup or 1 Cup Buttermilk (room temperature)

3 large eggs room temperature

3 oz red food coloring

2 tsp pure vanilla

1 Cup hot water + 1 Tbsp instant decaffeinated coffee + (4 Tbsp Chocolate Liqueur or extract)

3 Cups sweeten shredded coconut to line the sides of cake

1 small container of red sprinkles for top of cake

Cream Cheese Frosting:

1 lb or 2 (8oz) cream cheese softened

4 Cups confectioners' sugar

2 sticks or 1 Cup soften butter

2 tsp clear vanilla

Continued on next page

Preheat oven to 350° F (175° C).

Sift together the flour, sugar, baking soda, salt.

Using a standing mixer with bowl, mix together the oil, milk/vinegar mixture, eggs, food coloring, vanilla and hot water mixture plus cocoa until all ingredients are well combined.

Mix the dry ingredients in a separate bowl with a wire whisk then add to the wet ingredients third batch at a time until each batch is completely combined and batter is a consistence that is smooth red velvety texture about 4-5 minutes.

Divide the cake batter evenly among the prepared (<u>sprayed with oil and lined with parchment paper</u>) cake pans. Place cake pans in the oven on the top rack evenly spaced apart. Bake and rotate pans halfway through the cooking process until cake pulls away from the side of the pans and a toothpick inserted in the center of the cakes comes out clean about 30 – 45 minutes depending on what type of oven you have. I bake on convectional bake for 45 minutes and check half way through cooking process.

Remove cakes from the oven, cool slightly, and then run a knife around the edge to loosen them from the sides of the pans. One at a time invert the cakes onto a plate (remove paper) and then re-invert them onto a cooling rack, rounded sides up. Let cool completely.

Divide each cake into half by inserting a serrated knife through the center from side to side so it will be split into 2 round halves. Clean knife after each use.

In a mixer with a whisk attachment mix the cream cheese, sugar, and butter on low speed until incorporated. Increase speed to high and mix until light and fluffy about 2-5 minutes. Occasionally scrape down side of bowl with rubber spatula.

Reduce speed of the mixer to low add clear vanilla, raise speed to high and mix briefly until fluffy. Then store the frosting in the refrigerator until somewhat stiff. Maybe made ahead of time and stored in refrigerator up to 3 days.

Frost each layer with frosting spread enough frosting to make a 1/4 to 1/2" layer. Carefully set another layer on top rounded side down and repeat until all the layers are frosted and stacked on top of each other. Top with the remaining layer cover entire cake with remaining frosting. Sprinkle top heavily with red sprinkles and put coconut onto sides.

NOTES: *Very impressive looking cake for a holiday or any party. Inspired from a cake I ordered from California but the cake came shipped to me all smashed and broken so I decided to try and create my own version.*

SERVING SUGGESTIONS: If by any chance you have left over red velvet cake with frosting you can make **Red Velvet White Coconut Truffles** (great on Valentine's Day).

Mix the cake along with frosting in a large bowl thoroughly with your clean hands until it forms a dough. With your Mellon scooper form small red velvet balls and place onto a baking pan lined with parchment paper in to the freezer for about 30 minutes until hard set.

In a double boiler melt white coconut chocolate plus unsalted butter (every 10 oz use a 1/2 stick of unsalted butter or 1/4 Cup) to coat the red velvet balls. Place back onto parchment paper and back into freezer for another 30 minutes until hard set. Take back out and recoat the red velvet balls again and place onto parchment paper and back into freezer for another 30 minutes or until hard set.

Take out the red velvet truffles and let set for about an hour until soft; serve and enjoy.

BANANA FOSTER BREAD PUDDING

12 Servings
Prep time: 25 minutes Total time: 1 1/2 hours

Sweet, delectable dark chocolate and white coconut chocolate in a banana bread pudding with white cream sauce poured on top that will have you coming back for seconds.

9 Tbsp unsalted butter

2 Cups white graduated sugar

3/4 tsp ground cinnamon + 1 whole split vanilla bean

6 bananas peeled cut 1" round slices

1/2 Cup banana liqueur <u>or</u> 1 oz banana extract

1/2 Cup Dark Rum <u>or</u> 1 oz rum extract

8 Cups freshly ground all white bread crumbs

6 large eggs, lightly beaten

4 Cups heavy cream

3 oz or 96 grams dry banana cream pudding	1/8 tsp salt
3 oz or 96 grams dry pineapple jello mix	10 oz chopped chocolate dusted with flour (Dark Chocolate 70% Cocoa)
1 tsp pure vanilla extract	
1/8 tsp freshly grated nutmeg	10 oz chopped white coconut chocolate dusted with flour

Preheat oven to 350° F (175° C). Butter a 10 x 14" clear glass baking dish with a tablespoon of butter.

Melt the remaining 8 Tbsp butter in a large skillet over medium heat. Add 1 Cup of the sugar and the cinnamon, vanilla bean and cook, stirring, until the sugar dissolves, about 2 minutes. Add the bananas and cook on both sides, turning until the bananas start to soften and brown, about 3 minutes. Add the banana liqueur and stir to blend. Carefully add the rum and shake the pan back and forth to warm the rum and flame the pan or carefully ignite the rum with a match off the heat and then return to the heat when lit. Shake the pan back and forth or spoon liquid over bananas so as to baste them until the flame dies. Remove from the heat to cool. If using extracts once the bananas have soften and caramelized take off of heat and add extract and stir and cool.

Whisk together the eggs, remaining sugar, salt, heavy cream, dry pudding mix along with dry jello, vanilla, and nutmeg in a large bowl. Add the bread crumbs and stir to combined, fold in the cooled banana mixture, fold in the chopped chocolate (white and dark) and stir to blend thoroughly. Pour into the prepared baking dish and bake uncovered for about 45 minutes then cover and bake additional 10-20 minutes longer until firm in center. Cool slightly so as to be warm not hot.

Meanwhile you can make <u>Cream Sauce</u>:

2 Cups Heavy Cream + 1/2 Cup white Sugar <u>or</u> 2 Cups Vanilla Ice Cream
1 whole vanilla bean split and scraped
4-5 Tbsp dry vanilla pudding mix
4 Tbsp Dark Rum <u>or</u> 1 oz rum extract

In a small sauce pan over medium to low heat combine the cream, sugar and vanilla bean paste stir for about 5 minutes until it is just before boiling point. Add the dry pudding mix by stirring a tablespoon at a time to thicken sauce enough to have it run down the sides of bread pudding. Take off of heat and add the rum or extract and stir and serve immediately with bread pudding. If you like serve with Hazelnut ice cream too.

APPLE CHEESECAKE PUMPKIN PIE

1 (10" SPRING FORM PAN)
Prep time: 40 minutes Total Time: 3 hours

A trio that is "All American" as the song "Take Me Out to the Ball Game", rolled up into one complete dessert, (layered dessert assembled in a spring form pan). A flaky buttery pie crust for the bottom, plus a layer of graham cracker crust, then first starting with a pumpkin pie mixture, then a cheesecake mixture and finally the apple pie mixture layer. Then topped with strips of scalloped edged pie crust arranged in a diamond shape pattern.

Graham Cracker Crust: (for sides of pie)

2 Cups finely crushed graham crackers

1/2 Cup white sugar

1/2 Cup butter melted

2 prepared 9" pie dough rolled

Pumpkin Pie Layer:

3/4 Cup granulated sugar

1 tsp ground cinnamon

1/2 tsp salt

1/4 tsp ground ginger

1/8 tsp ground cloves

1 tsp pumpkin pie spice (cinn, ginger, nutmeg, allspice)

2 Large eggs

1 can (15 oz) pure pumpkin (2 Cups prepared pumpkin)

1 can (12 oz) evaporated milk

Cheesecake Layer:

16 oz soften cream cheese

1 Cup (226 grams) granulated white sugar

1 tsp pure vanilla

2 large eggs

Apple Pie Layer:

2 1/2 pounds (1.1 kg) apples (about 6 large), peeled cored, and sliced 1" thick (about 8 Cups sliced) (about 900 grams sliced)

1/4 Cup granulated white sugar

1/4 Cup light brown sugar

1 tsp lemon juice

1 tsp ground cinnamon

1/4 tsp ground nutmeg

1/4 tsp salt

2 Tbsp unsalted butter

3.4 oz (96grams) vanilla instant pudding powder

Preheat oven to 425° F (220° C).

To prepare the graham cracker crust in a food processor pulse your ingredients together until it forms dough like consistence. Take out of food processor and press firmly into sides of spring form pan (sprayed w/oil) so it goes completely up the sides all around to cover all sides about 1/8"thick. Take one prepared pie crust and fit into pan to overlap the graham cracker crust and press firmly against the side to adhere to the graham cracker crust and press out any air bubbles that have trapped on bottom.

Next to prepare the pumpkin pie, mix sugar, cinnamon, salt, ginger, cloves, and pumpkin pie spice in a small bowl. Beat eggs in large bowl and stir in pumpkin and sugar-spice mixture. Gradually stir in evaporated milk.

Pour into a spring form pan with graham cracker crust and pie crust. Set aside for later.

Now prepare the cheesecake layer by mixing cream cheese, sugar and vanilla with mixer on medium speed until well blended. Add eggs one at a time, mix until blended. Pour on top of pumpkin pie and carefully spread out the cheese mixture evenly on top (cheesecake layer will rise to top when baked).

Put into the preheated oven on a baking sheet and bake for about 15 - 25 minutes until crust forms on cheese cake then reduce the temperature of the oven to 350° F (175° C) by leaving the door of your oven open until it reached desired temperature. Close the oven door and bake for another 55-60 minutes until center is set. Cool for at least 2 hours until center had hardened enough to put apple pie layer on top. Also if pie has not cooled enough put into refrigerator for another hour and then it will be ready for apple pie layer.

The last layer is the apple pie layer; in a large bowl or plastic gallon sized bag combine the sliced apples, sugars, lemon juice, ground cinnamon, nutmeg, and salt. Place in a large sauce pan on stove top over a medium heat, add butter and cook until apples are soften enough to eat about 20-25 minutes. Then add the pudding powder to thicken the sauce and stir to combine completely. Pour apple mixture on top of cooled cheesecake and set aside.

Now with the other rolled out pie crust using a scalloped edge cutter cut strips of dough about 1" in width and lay the strips on top of apple pie diagonal to form a diamond shape centers so as to see some of the apple pie mixture exposed as shown in picture. Trim off sides that have overlapping pie crust and brush with egg wash.

Place in oven under your broiler about 5" from boiler at 400° F (205° C) for 10-15 minutes rotating every 2-5 minutes until the crust is golden.

Take out of oven and let cool for about 30 minutes and remove from spring form pan and cut and serve with ice cream or whipped cream.

TIP: Any dry cookies you like crushed can be used for outer crust instead of graham cracker. Pumpkin/cheesecake layers can be made one day ahead and stored in refrigerator, take out 1 hour before serving and add the apple layer.

NOTES: *This was inspired for my husband on Father's Day. These are his favorite desserts all rolled up into one happy family. A great hit at a Fourth of July Party or for Thanksgiving Day!*

Suzanne Schwendiman

CHOCOLATE SODA BREAD WITH VANILLA/BOURBON SAUCE

8 SERVINGS
Prep time: 15 minutes Total time: 80 minutes

Cake like bread that acts and taste like cake because of its chocolaty taste and a vanilla sweet cream sauce poured over the top to soak into every nook and crannies of the bread.

Preheat oven to 350° F (175° C). Spray a large glass bread pan with oil to grease pan.

In a mixing bowl using a whisk combine flour sugar, baking powder, baking soda, salt, and cocoa powder. In another mixing bowl with electric mixer blend eggs, buttermilk and sour cream. Mix the liquid mixture into flour mixture 1/3 batch at a time until fully combined about 2-4 minutes. Pour the combined batter into the greased bread pan. Bake in the preheated oven for about 65 minutes until center is set and sides of bread start to pull away from pan. Let cool and turn bread out onto a wire rack.

Bread:	Sauce:
2 Cups granulated white sugar	2 Cups heavy cream
4 Cups all purpose white flour	1 whole vanilla bean split and scraped seed into cream
3 tsp baking powder	3-4 Tbsp vanilla pudding dry mix to thicken sauce
1 tsp baking soda	
1/4 tsp salt	4 Tbsp sugar or more to taste
8 Tbsp dark Dutch Process cocoa powder	1/4 Cup bourbon liquor or 1 oz bourbon extract
2 large eggs beaten	
1 1/2 Cups Buttermilk	
1 Cup sour cream	

In a medium sauce pan heat cream to warm about 200° F (95° C), add vanilla bean and seeds scraped from pod, dry pudding mix, sugar and stir until fully combined. You will know it is ready when the vanilla bean is well incorporated and you can smell the aroma of the vanilla. Take off of stove top then add your bourbon, stir to combine.

Slice bread about 1" thick. Serve bread warm topped with warm vanilla sauce.

NOTES: *This was inspired from eating at an Irish Pub and it was a special dessert that day and never to be served again until I came up with my own version of it.*

CHOCOLATE SOUFFLÉ WITH CRÈME ANGLAISE

4 Servings
Prep time: 20 minutes Total time: 40 minutes

<u>SOUFFLÉ:</u> Preheat oven to 375° F (190° C).

Butter soufflé dishes or ramekins and dust with a little sugar. Tilt and tap out excess sugar.

In medium saucepan, combine milk and 1 1/4 Cups sugar and bring to a boil.

In a small saucepan, over medium heat, melt butter and slowly mix in flour. Then stir in milk mixture. Slowly cook over low temperature, until mixture pulls from the saucepan, about 5 minutes. Do not boil.

Remove from heat add cocoa and stir, slowly add egg yolks, one at a time until well incorporated, then orange zest and Grand Marnier and stir to incorporate all ingredients. Set aside.

In a mixing bowl, beat egg whites and cream of tartar, salt with an electric mixer on medium speed until eggs are frothy. Increase speed to high and gradually add the other 1/4 Cup of sugar, beating egg whites until they form soft peaks.

Spoon 1/2 of egg whites into the Grand Marnier mixture then gently fold in the egg whites into the mixture until the batter is lightened. Fold in remaining egg whites, taking care not to deflate them. Divide the mixture into the soufflé dishes and arrange on a baking sheet pan.

Bake for about 25 minutes or until the soufflés have doubled in size and have a slight firm crust on top.

CRÈME ANGLAISE: Prepare cream Anglaise by mixing egg yolks with sugar. Bring milk and pre-cut vanilla bean to a boil, and then slowly stir milk mixture into egg mixture couple tablespoon at a time at first so as not to curd the egg. Gently simmer the mixture for about 10 minutes or until cream coats the back of a wooden spoon. Do not allow sauce to boil. Now stir in honey and almond extract. Take out vanilla bean. Remove from heat, pour into a bowl, and stir for a minute or two to cool.

Dust the soufflés with powdered sugar and serve immediately with crème anglaise.

Soufflé:

1 1/4 Cup milk
1/2 Cup white granulated sugar
5 Tbsp unsalted butter
1/2 Cup all-purpose flour, sifted
6 egg yolks
1/4 Cup Dark Dutch Process Cocoa
Zest of half an orange
2 Tbsp grand Marnier/orange extract
8 egg whites
1 tsp cream of tartar
1/8 tsp salt
1/4 Cup sugar

Crème Anglaise:

6 egg yolks
1/2 Cup white granulated sugar
1 1/2 Cups milk
2 Tbsp Honey
1 Tbsp Almond extract
1 vanilla bean, split lengthwise or 1 Tbsp vanilla extract

Garnish:

1/2 Cup powdered sugar

CARAMEL APPLE PIE WITH SHORTBREAD CRUST

8-10 Servings
Prep Time: 1 hour Total Time: 3 hours

What makes this a unique apple pie is first it is baked in a paper bag and has a delicious golden shortbread crust on top with a heavenly caramel sauce that just keeps you wanting more.

Preheat oven to 375° F (190° C).

Bottom Crust: One 9 inch deep dish pie pan sprayed with oil and carefully put one premade crust in bottom gently pushing crust up the sides of pan. Next put the other premade crust on top of the first premade crust and gently push to sides and up. Pierce crust with a fork all over to prevent air pockets in crust.

Apple Filling: Put all apples into a large zip lock gallon bag and coat well with flour and pepper. Pour over premade crust and sprinkle brown sugar on top.

Caramel Sauce: Over low heat in a small sauce pan add in white sugar until melts (if sugar starts to burn before it melts add the water), and then add cinnamon stick until sugar caramelizes to a dark rich brown color about 2-3 minutes. Add in the nutmeg, Kahlua, butter and ice cream; stir after each ingredient is added until fully incorporated over low heat. Take out cinnamon stick and pour immediately over apple filling.

Shortbread Crust: (make ahead of time and stored in refrigerator, take out and let dough soften just enough to work with) Mix all ingredients together in a standing mixer, fitted with dough hook, on low for about 2-4 minutes until dough forms and is fully incorporated. Split dough into half and roll out half for pie crust 1/4" thick. Put crust on top of apple filling (if crust falls apart just patch it on the apple filling). (Cutouts are Optional) Second half roll out about 1/8" thick for mini apple and oak leaf cookie cutters to cut out. I cut out 40 mini apples and 80 mini leaves to cover up patched shortbread crust. Bake apple pie without mini cookies in a paper bag folded over on a sheet pan for about 1 hour in a preheated oven. Take out of oven and cut bag completely open to expose the entire top of pie, bush crust with egg wash. Then add apple cut outs by placing on top center of pie, then around sides and down to edge of pie pan place the leaf cut outs. Brush again with egg wash and put back into oven at 350° F (175° C) until golden brown 15–30 minutes, then turn off oven. You may leave pie in oven up to 4 hours before serving warm with vanilla ice cream on the side.

Shortbread Crust:

4 stick of butter (1lb or 453.62 grams)

4 Cups all purpose flour

2 Cups granulated white sugar

Bottom Crust:

2 premade pie crust dough

1 egg plus 2 TBSP water beaten together for egg wash

Caramel Sauce:

1 Cup white granulated sugar

1/3 Cup water if sugar starts to burn

1 stick of cinnamon

1/8 tsp freshly grated nutmeg

1/2 stick of unsalted butter (1/4 Cup)

1/2 Cup French Vanilla Kahlua or French Vanilla Coffee Syrups

1/2 Cup Vanilla Ice Cream

Apple Filling:

10 large or 20 small peeled cored granny smith apples

1/2 Cup all purpose white flour

1/8 tsp cayenne pepper

1/2 Cup light brown sugar

PEAR TART WITH CRUMB CAKE TOPPING

12 Servings
Prep time: 20 minutes Total time 2 hours

This tart has a uniquely thick layer of buttery, flaky crust fused together with a thin layer of cheesecake. On top of the cheese cake is a layer of roasted pears with a Caramel sauce drizzled over top. The top crust is a crumb crust of cheese cake, pound cake, sugar and cinnamon mixed together.

Preheat oven to 400° F (205° C).

Roast pears in a glass baking pan with sliced stick of butter, 1 lemon juiced, 3/4 Cup vanilla sugar (put split vanilla bean into sugar incorporate until you see black specks) and 1/2 cup Kahlua to sliced pears in a preheated oven for about 25 -30 minutes until soft.

Meanwhile beat 1 Cup sugar and eggs together until well mixed. Add soften cream cheese and mix until fully incorporated and then add 1 lemon juiced plus zest, mix for another minute. Pour a thin layer (1/4" thick) into tart pan with pie crust firmly packed down into pan. Bake for about 10-15 minutes in a 425° F (220° C) oven until crust is formed on top reduce oven temperature to 350° F (175° C) by leaving oven door open until temperature reaches 350° F (175° C). Cook for another 10-15 minutes until cheesecake is set firmly through center.

1 (10" pie crust) 1/4" thick or 2 (9") premade pie crust thaw and rolled out together to fit tart pan	2 Cups granulated white sugar
1 tart pan with a center that removes	1/2 Cup French Vanilla Kahlua or French Vanilla Coffee Syrup
5 large pears peeled and 1/4" sliced	16 oz softened cream cheese
1 vanilla beans split seeds removed	2 large eggs
2 lemons juiced plus zest of one	1 (store bought) vanilla pound cake
1/2 Stick unsalted butter (1/4 Cup)	2 tsp cinnamon

Pour remaining cheese mixture into a well greased pan lined with parchment paper and cook in the oven at the same time and temperature as cheese tart. This remaining cheesecake is for crumb topping.

Cool cheesecake for about 1 hour or until firmly set (refrigerate if need be). Add roasted pears to top of tart in a circular fanned fashion. Pour remaining juice from roasting pears into a small sauce pan over high heat and reduce to a dark Caramel sauce about 10 minutes then drizzle over top of fanned pears.

Crumble pound cake and remaining cooked cheesecake together along with a 1/4 Cup sugar, 2 tsp cinnamon in a small bowl mix until well incorporated with wire whisk. Sprinkle over top of pear tart and refrigerate for 1 hour and serve with a side of vanilla ice cream.

TIP: For an even quicker version omit making cheesecake and buy a good store bought cheesecake that is already made. Bake your crust (pierced with fork add in baking beans to weigh down crust) for about 10 minutes in a 400° F (205° C) oven. Let crust cool to room temperature and crumble half of store bought cheese cake into tart crust and then follow directions to roasting pears and fanning out pears and making the caramel sauce and then adding cake crumble topping with the other half of store bought cheese cake.

NOTES: *Inspired from a NYC restaurant I had dinner at. A version of this pear tart was served.*

CHOCOLATE COVERED ANGEL FOOD CAKE

8-10 Servings
Prep Time: 15 minutes Total Time: 2 hours

This cake has a moist, tender, not overly sweet and very light texture. It has a unique flavor combination of pure vanilla and almond that nicely complement each other. What finishes this so nicely is a thick drizzle of chocolate ganache. (Picture shown has white coconut chocolate swirls in the milk chocolate topping)

<u>Cake:</u>	<u>Chocolate Ganache:</u>
16 extra large egg whites <u>OR</u>	**1/2 lb semisweet chocolate chips**
12 extra large egg whites plus	**3/4 Cup heavy cream**
2/3 Cup liquid egg whites	
1 1/2 Cups superfine white sugar	
1 Cup sifted cake flour	
1 1/2 tsp cream of tartar	
1/2 tsp salt	
2 tsp clear vanilla extract	
2 tsp pure almond oil extract	

Preheat oven to 325° F (165° C).

In a small bowl, whisk together 3/4 Cup of sugar and the cake flour, set aside.

In a separate large mixing bowl beat egg whites until frothy, then add cream of tartar and salt. Beat until fully incorporated then begin to add the remaining 1/4 Cup of sugar 1 to 2 tablespoons at a time. When sugar has been added, beat egg whites to soft peaks you will know when you have soft peaks because the egg whites will look like soft waves and when you lift the beaters, the peaks will drop back down into the batter. If your batter is falling in ribbons, it is not quite done. Don't be afraid to slow down the mixer and check a few times as you get close. Do not beat all the way to stiff peaks. Once you have soft peaks, add the vanilla and almond extracts and beat for a few more minutes to evenly distribute until stiffer peaks form. Sift 1/4 of the flour/sugar mixture over the egg whites and gently fold it very carefully into the batter with a rubber spatula. Continue adding the flour/sugar mixture in 3 equal additions, sifting and folding until it's

130

all incorporated (just until ribbon of flour/sugar mixture is covered). It is better to take your time and do it gently than to rush and deflate the egg whites. Pour batter into a lightly sprayed with oil 10" tube cake pan with a removable bottom. Smooth the top with a spatula and tap the pan on the counter once or twice to ensure that there are no large bubbles lurking beneath the surface. Bake for about 50-55 minutes until the top springs back when lightly pressed. Remove from oven and invert the pan on a cooling rack. When cool, run a thin, flexible knife around the cake to remove it from the pan.

For the chocolate ganache place the chocolate chips and the heavy cream in a heat proof bowl over a pan of simmering water and stir until the chocolate melts. Pour the chocolate over the top of the cooled cake to cover the top completely and allow it to heavily drizzle down the sides and center of cake. Let chocolate cool and harden about 15 minutes, cut and serve.

NOTES: *Definitely worth the effort instead of store bought.* **TIP:** *Can't find superfine sugar process granulated white sugar in a food processor until superfine for about one minute.*

HEAVENLY COCONUT POUND CAKE

1 TUBE CAKE PAN
Prep Time: 20 minutes Total time: 2 hours

This cake is light and fluffy and it has a heavenly sweet taste. It is finished off with a coconut butter cream icing drizzled over the top that resembles white clouds.

Preheat oven to 350° F (175° C). Spray with oil to grease the tube cake pan.

In the bowl of your electric mixer beat the butter until creamy and smooth. Gradually add the sugar, beating continuously on medium speed until light and fluffy about 2 minutes. Scrape down the sides of the bowl as needed. After about 2 minutes the batter should be light in color and fluffy in texture. Then add the egg yolks, one at a time, mixing well after each addition until pale in color, light and fluffy texture. Add your coconut oil and mix to combine. Scrape down the sides of the bowl as needed. Whisk together in a separate bowl flour, baking powder and salt and add it to liquid mixture 1/3 batch at a time, alternating with the buttermilk until fully combined about 5 minutes. Then add your vanilla, almond, coconut, butter, rum extract and lemon, orange extracts to batter until thorough mixed together about 1 minute.

Beat egg whites in separate bowl using electric mixer on high speed to soft peaks about 2 minutes. Then gently fold the egg whites into the cake batter using a rubber spatula for about 1 minute until the egg whites are fully incorporated, this will give the cake a light and fluffy texture.

Pour cake mixture into greased cake pan then smooth out the top using a rubber spatula and tap on counter to release any air bubbles. Then put into a preheated oven for about 90-95 minutes until golden brown and toothpick or knife comes out clean. Start checking on cake after about 75 minutes into the baking process and cover top of cake with foil so to stop browning of the crust. Take out of oven and let pan cool about 20 minutes, then gently insert knife around edges and the center of pan, then invert onto a wire rack to finish cooling.

For the icing combine the sugar and butter in a mixing bowl and beat until completely combined. Slowly add the milk to thin out the icing enough so as to drizzle down the cake sides when poured over the cake, then add the coconut extract stir to combine fully. Frost the cake and let icing harden; cut and serve.

TIPS: Cannot find cake flour add 1/4 Cup of cornstarch to 1 ¾ Cup all-purpose white flour which yields 2 Cups of cake flour or put 2 Tablespoons into bottom of 1 cup measuring cup and add the flour to have one cup of cake flour then be sure to sift this together.

Cake:

3 Cups granulated white sugar

2 stick (226 grams) unsalted butter softened

5 large eggs room temperature separated

1/4 Cup extra virgin coconut oil
(room temperature liquid form)

1 Cup buttermilk room temperature

3 Cups cake flour

2 tsp baking powder

1/4 tsp salt

2 tsp pure vanilla

2 tsp pure almond oil extract

2 tsp pure coconut oil extract

2 tsp butter extract

2 tsp rum extract

Coconut Butter Cream Icing:

1 Cup powdered sugar (115 grams)

1/2 stick of unsalted butter softened or
1/4 Cup (56.7 grams)

1/4 Cup milk more or less to thin out the icing

1 tsp coconut oil extract

PASSION CAKE

2 (9" ROUNDS)
Prep Time: 30 minutes Total Time: 1 hour

Dense, moist cake with royal cheesecake frosting. To embellish the look, orange and green icing was added to the top of cake to resemble carrots. This recipe can also be made into passion truffles which make great gifts.

Cake:

2 Cups light brown sugar

4 large eggs room temperature

1 1/2 Cups Extra Virgin Coconut Oil room temp

3 Cups grated carrots

1 tsp pure vanilla

2 tsp rum extract or 2 Tbsp rum liqueur

1 tsp salt

2 tsp cinnamon

1/2 tsp nutmeg

2 Cups unbleached all purpose white flour

2 tsp baking soda

1/2 Cup finely chopped nuts (pecans)

Royal Cheesecake Icing:

2 large egg whites

2 tsp fresh lemon juice

16 oz softened cream cheese

5 Cups powdered sugar (add 1 Cup at a time to reach

desired spreading consistency)

1 oz orange extract

<u>Carrot Designs:</u> (Optional use leftover icing)

orange gel food coloring

green gel food coloring

Preheat oven temperature to 350° F (175° C) and spray with oil 2 (9") cake pans.

Combine sugar and eggs with electric mixer until fluffy about 1-2 minutes. Then add oil (bring oil to a liquid form by heating it if it is solid), carrots, vanilla, and rum and blend to combine thoroughly.

Sift together in a separate bowl salt, baking soda and flour. Then add to the flour mixture your cinnamon and nutmeg by whisking together.

Add the dry ingredients 1/3 batch at a time until each dry batch has been thoroughly combined about 2-4 minutes.

Fold nuts into batter.

Pour cake batter evenly into prepared (sprayed with oil, **lined with parchment paper**) cake pans and tap on counter to release any bubbles that may have occurred. Bake cake pans for about 35-40 minutes until cake center springs back and sides of cake has started to come away from the pans.

Cool cakes about 2-3 hours on cake racks. Assemble cakes first by frosting in between layer about 1/4" thick layer and then placing round sides together and frost top and sides with Royal Cheesecake Icing and decorate with carrot designs. This next step is optional but well worth the effort because how all the

ingredients have time to infuse together to produce a very moist and dense cake. Put cake into a plastic cake container sealed and put into refrigerator for 24 or 48 hours to have frosting fused together with cake. Cake will last anywhere to several days up to a week in air tight cake container in refrigerator.

Royal Cheesecake Icing using a mixing bowl of your electric mixer beat the egg whites with lemon juice until foam forms. Combine the softened cream cheese, orange extract and then add the sifted powdered sugar one cup at a time and beat on low speed until combined and smooth. The icing needs to be used immediately or transferred to an airtight container so the icing can have a stiffer consistency. Cover with plastic wrap when not in use while spreading. For carrot designs using some of the left over icing add a little orange gel to reach desired orange color for the carrot and place into a plastic bag with corner end snipped off for exposure for piping. For the green stem using some of the left over white icing; add a little green gel to reach desired color for the stems of carrots and add to another plastic bag and snip off corner end for exposing icing so as to pipe next to carrots.

SERVING SUGGESTIONS: If by any chance you have left over passion cake with frosting you can make Passion White Coconut Truffles (great for gifts).

Mix the cake along with frosting in a large bowl thoroughly with your clean hands until it forms dough. With your Mellon scooper or your clean hands form small passion cake balls and place onto a baking pan lined with parchment paper in to the freezer for about 30 minutes until hard set.

In a double boiler melt white coconut chocolate plus unsalted butter (every 10 oz use a 1/2 stick of unsalted butter or 1/4 Cup) to coat the passion cake balls. Place back onto parchment paper and back into freezer for another 30 minutes until hard set. Take back out and recoat the passion cake balls again and place onto parchment paper and back into freezer for another 30 minutes or until hard set.

Take out the passion truffles and let set until soft about an hour; serve and enjoy.

NOTES: *Inspired from a bakery I fell in love with where I grew up that no longer serves this original recipe. Thank goodness I came up with my own original recipe that is just as good.*

TIP: Instead of Royal Cheesecake icing buy a good store brand of White Cream Cheese Frosting.

Everything Else

BOLOGNESE TOMATO SAUCE

1 GALLON
Prep Time: 20 minutes Total Time: 90 minutes

*Using the finest and freshest ingredients will give your sauce a wonderful delicious flavor
along with a wonderful aroma.*

**12 Fire Roasted Whole Tomatoes (skins removed)
Or 3(28 oz) can whole peeled organic tomatoes
(Use one or the other or a combination of both
depending on what you can find)**

4 Tbsp extra virgin olive oil

1 whole carrot minced

1 yellow onion minced

1 celery stock minced

6 cloves garlic minced

2 Tbsp Liquid Amino

2 lbs freshly ground chop steak

1 lb ground bison (can't find use more steak)

3 Tbsp Chicken Bouillon Base

1/4 Cup fresh basil chopped or 1 Tbsp Dried basil

3 Tbsp dried oregano (crushed in palm)

1 tsp dried Thyme (crushed in palm)

1 Tbsp onion power

1 Tbsp garlic powder

Salt & fresh ground black pepper to taste

In a large cast iron frying pan or large sauce pan over medium to high heat add oil, minced vegetables (carrot, onion, celery and garlic) sauté until soft about 1-2 minutes then add the ground meat and the liquid amino plus fresh ground black pepper to taste. Breaking up the ground meat with the back of spoon as it cooks so it will be into very small pieces until browned completely about 10 minutes. Crush your tomatoes with clean hands inside of the can and add to brown meat mixture. Stir to incorporate all the ingredients and simmer for about 1 hour until sauce thickens. Once sauce is thickened add dried oregano and thyme (add dried basil if that is what your using too) crushed in palm to release the aroma then add the onion, garlic powder, salt and pepper to taste cooking and stirring for another 10 minutes to combine all the seasonings. Just before serving turn heat off and stir in your fresh chopped basil.

TIP: Serve this sauce over my Homemade Pesto Pasta recipe found under section Pasta, Rice & Grains. Also for a time saver I chop the vegetables in the food processor until it is a fine paste.

NOTES: *Inspired from my family's love for a good meat sauce.*

Suzanne Schwendiman

PEACH MARMALADE

20 PINT SIZE JARS
Prep Time: 30 minutes Total Time: 1 hour

This marmalade goes fantastically in salad dressing, sauces and marinades.

2 dozen fresh peeled and pitted peaches (from your local peach farm)
3 Cups granulated white sugar
6 oz dry peach gelatin
1 lemon juiced plus zest
2 medium oranges juiced plus zest

On top of the stove, over medium heat, in a medium to large sauce pan, cook peaches until boiling and peaches are soft. Add your sugar, lemon, and oranges (without seeds). Stir to combine completely until sugar is dissolved. Turn heat to low and with hand held blender on low blend until chucky smooth so as to see a few chucks left. Add gelatin and stir until completely dissolved for another 5 minutes until marmalade is boiling. Turn off heat and let cool for about a minute.
Pour into prepared mason jam jars and seal. (Heat from the marmalade will seal the Mason jar lid when placed on).

NOTES: *This is a great way to have those fresh from the vine peach taste all year round in your favorite sauces, marinades and on top of your favorite fresh bread. This recipe can be substituted for any fresh in season fruit you like besides peaches etc. apricots, strawberry, blueberries, be sure to use the appropriate gelatin for the type of fruit you choose.*

BASIL PESTO SAUCE

3 CUPS
Prep Time: 10 minutes Total Time: 10 minutes

2 large bunches fresh basil (about 5-6 Cups chopped)	3/4 Cup Pine nuts
6 garlic cloves smashed with knife	2 lemons zest with juice
1/2 Cup extra virgin olive oil	2 tsp fresh ground black pepper
1/2 Cup Parmesan Cheese	2 tsp salt

Combine cut fresh basil and garlic into a food processor until well chopped. Add cheese, pine nuts, lemon with zest and salt and pepper, turn food processor back on and pour into spout of food processor oil until fully incorporated.

TIP: Can be put into homemade pasta recipe when making (see Pasta, Rice & Grain section for recipe); Also a great sauce for grilled flank steak, shrimp, fish and chicken. I even spread this sauce on my grilled Panini sandwiches. Sauce can keep in refrigerator up to a week or in freezer for longer. Instead of using basil you can use fresh cut <u>flat leaf parsley</u> in this recipe. I even put half basil and half parsley to this recipe and it still is a great pesto sauce for many uses.

NOTES: *Inspired from having a square foot garden with fresh basil growing and my neighbors love for this basil pesto sauce.*

TOMATO BASIL VINEGARETTE DRESSING

6 CUPS
Prep Time: 5 minutes Total Time: 5 minutes

The tomato dressing has a fresh from the garden taste with a hint of fresh sweet basil.

1 packet of Zesty Italian Dressing
1/2 Cup cold pressed extra virgin olive oil
1/2 Cup grape seed oil

1/4 Cup red wine/apple cider vinegar (mix the two vinegars)
1 (32 oz) can Fire Roasted Tomatoes
1/4 Cup fresh chopped basil

Combine all ingredients except basil in food processor until pureed.

Just before serving pulse the basil in the food processor until combined with dressing.

Store in an air tight container in refrigerator if not in use.

TIP: Substitute Zesty Italian packet, olive oil, grape seed oil, and vinegar for 2 cups of favorite prepared zesty Italian dressing in a bottle. To make it creamy add about ¼ cup heavy cream or plain fat free Greek yogurt to dressing.

Notes: *This dressing is my signature dressing for my seafood salad recipe found under Soup/Salad section.*

Suzanne Schwendiman

CITRUS SALAD DRESSING

24 oz
Prep time: 5 minutes Total Time: 5 minutes

This dressing goes great with my "Fresh Summer Salad" recipe found under the chapter entitled Soups & Salads.

1 (16oz) Zesty Italian prepared dressing
1/2 Cup fresh squeezed orange plus zest from oranges
1/4 Cup fresh squeezed lime juice plus the zest from the lime
3 Tbsp Honey
2 tsp freshly grated ginger

Combine all ingredients in a bowl, whisk together. Put into a dressing container and can be stored in the refrigerator up to a week.

Serve chilled with my Fresh Summer Salad.

VEAL & CHICKEN STOCK

6 CUPS
Prep Time: 10 minutes Total Time: 1 hours

8 Cups water

2 veal chop bones/scraps

1 whole chicken bones/scraps

1 peeled diced carrot

3 large celery stalks diced plus leaves

1 small yellow onion chopped

1 whole floret of garlic

Put all ingredients in a large size soup pot over medium to low heat for about 1 hours or until soup has reduced down to one cup. Cool slightly and separate both with strainer from ingredients by running broth through strainer.

Ready to be used in your soups or gravy, can be stored in an air tight container in the refrigerator for up to a week.

Suzanne Schwendiman

WHOLE WHEAT PIZZA DOUGH

1 LB
Prep time: 15 minutes Total time: 2 hours

This pizza dough recipe goes very well with my thin crust pizza recipe.

3 Cups fresh ground white wheat (gives the crust a crunchier texture & flour is very warm for dough)

2 tsp dry yeast

1/2 tsp salt

1 Cup warm water

2 Tbsp extra virgin olive oil

Combine all ingredients into your standing mixer fitted with dough hook attachment and bowl. Mix for about 5 minutes until dough forms and is well kneaded. (If using a biga mix into the dough the biga until well kneaded if desired)

Place dough in a well oiled large mixing bowl covered with plastic wrap for about 1 hour until doubled in size. Fold dough over and form 1 lb rounds dusted with flour let rest 20 minutes.

Roll out on to a well floured surface. Top with your favorite toppings.

TIP: Dough can be put in to a one gallon size plastic bag and kept in the refrigerator for up to a week. About 2 hours for using take out of refrigerator and place onto counter to become room temperature and easier to work with. I really don't worry about proofing my yeast for this recipe because I use this for my thin crust pizza so I prefer it to be as thin as I can get it. I first cook the dough slightly after rolling out as thin as possible then I add my desired toppings. For a chewy crust start one day before with a biga. Biga recipe is 1 ½ cups unbleached white flour 1 cup warm water and ¼ tsp of yeast. Mix the yeast into the water. Mix the water in the flour until the dough just forms. Leave in a covered bowl overnight at room temperature for 12 to 48 hours. Mix the biga into the above recipe.

NOTES: *This recipe was inspired because I like to eat healthier by using fresh ingredients. Shelf life for flour is not very long even if kept in refrigerator/freezer, so I like to grind it right before I use it. Try it and you will see the difference. I have always believed the fresher the better.*

MUSHROOM PESTO SAUCE

2 CUPS
Prep Time: 10 minutes Total Time: 20 minutes

This pesto sauce consists of a Sauté buttery porcini, shitake, cremini, and button mushrooms combination so as to form a delectable buttery and cheese paste.

2/3 oz dried porcini mushrooms
(Soaked in 1 cup hot water for 10 min)

6 Shitake mushrooms cleaned stem removed
sliced

10 cremini (baby portabella) sliced

10 button mushrooms sliced

1/4 Cup unsalted butter (1/2 stick)

Salt and fresh ground black pepper to taste
about 1/2 tsp of each

1/4 Cup finely chopped fresh parsley

1/2 Cup Parmesan Cheese

2 garlic cloves minced

1 small yellow onion diced

1 Tbsp fresh squeezed lemon juice

Heat butter in a skillet over moderate heat until foam subsides, then add all mushrooms without liquid, onions, garlic cook until mushrooms are dry and darker about 5 minutes. Add reserve liquid; cook another 10 minutes until liquid is mostly absorbed.

In a food processor pour cooled mushroom mixture, add parsley, cheese, lemon juice, salt and pepper; pulse until very finely chopped into a paste.

TIP: May use just grilled portabella mushrooms or any style that are available to you at your local market. Serve over garlic chive toast for an appetizer or you can use this pesto to top the filet in my Puffed Pastry Wrapped Filet Mignon recipe found under chapter entitled "Meat & Poultry" section.

Suzanne Schwendiman

SUZANNE'S GREEN GODDESS DRESSING

40 OZ
Prep Time: 10 minutes Total Time: 40 minutes

This dressing has a fresh from the garden taste of English cucumber, dill and chives smoothly blended with a thick creamy Greek yogurt and mayonnaise.

1 large bunch fresh chives (about 1 Cup)

1 large bunch fresh dill (about 1 Cup)

1 Lemon zest plus juiced

2 Tbsp extra virgin olive oil (or any good oil used in dressings)

1 large English Cucumber (seeds removed using tsp) then diced

32 oz fat free plain Greek Yogurt

1 Cup fat free <u>or</u> real mayonnaise

3 tsp salt or to taste

4 tsp freshly ground pepper or to taste

Place chives, dill, oil, zest and lemon juice into food processor until it looks like pesto or until well minced about 2-3 minutes. Pour chive mixture in a large mixing bowl combine diced cucumber, yogurt, mayonnaise, salt and pepper to taste. Pulse with a handheld blender until thick and smooth with a few small pieces of cucumber still in dressing; add more salt and pepper to taste.

Pour dressing in air tight sealed container and placed into refrigerator for about 30 minutes to marinade all the flavors.

TIP: This dressing taste the freshest when used the same day as made; but can be kept up to a week in refrigerator but loses some of it fresh taste. Great used over rotisserie chicken on a whole wheat pita garnished with a few diced purple onions and diced tomatoes.

NOTES: *This recipe is a spin off from my Cucumber Dill Dressing; has almost the same ingredients but yields totally different results and tastes. It is the process in how everything is put together.*

CUCUMBER DILL DRESSING

32 OZ
Prep Time: 10 minutes Total Time: 40 minutes

This dressing resembles a cool and refreshing summer day of fresh dill, chives and English cucumber combination that enlightens the taste buds.

16 oz Greek Plain Fat Free Yogurt (water drained off)
1/2 Cup Fat Free <u>or</u> real mayonnaise
1 large bunch of dill chopped (about 1 Cup)
1 large bunch of chives chopped (about 1 Cup)
1 English cucumber (seeds removed with tsp) then diced
Salt and fresh ground black pepper to taste

Place all ingredients into a large mixing bowl, puree using a handheld blender until smoothly combined or pulse in a food processor.

Place dressing in an air tight container in refrigerator for 30 minutes before using.

TIP: This dressing is great as a dip for your favorite pita bread or your favorite fresh vegetables, over a fresh salad with chicken on top.

NOTES: *Freshly cut ingredients from your square foot garden will make this dressing the best you have ever tasted.*

FINISHING BBQ SAUCE

32 OZ
Prep Time: 10 minutes Total Time: 15 minutes

*Rich Sweet Hickory Smoked flavored barbecue sauce good on my tenderloin recipe,
rotisserie chicken or even on your favorite burger.*

1 1/4 Cups Molasses

**3/4 Cup homemade peach marmalade
(See recipe in this section)**

3/4 Cup Honey

3/4 Cup Yellow Mustard

3/4 Cup Ketchup

5 Tbsp White Vinegar

1/8 tsp cayenne pepper

6 Tbsp liquid hickory smoke

6 Tbsp brown sugar

2 Tbsp smoked paprika

1 Tbsp onion powder

1 Tbsp garlic powder

6 oz tomato paste

Combine all ingredients into a small sauce pan over medium heat stirring until sauce thickens about 15 minutes.

When not using, store in an air-tight container in the refrigerator for another recipe.

MUSTARD DILL SAUCE

2 CUPS
Prep Time: 5 minutes Total Time: 30 minutes

This sauce is so great on salmon or in my salmon quiche recipe. I was inspired to embellish the flavor of a good piece of salmon.

1/4 Cup fresh dill chopped
1/4 Cup course ground mustard or yellow mustard
1/2 Cup plain fat free yogurt or regular plain yogurt
1/2 Cup fat free mayonnaise or real mayonnaise
Salt & Pepper to taste

In medium bowl mix all ingredients together with a whisk for about 1-2 minutes so everything is well incorporated.

Store in an air tight container in the refrigerator for up to 30 minutes prior to serving over salmon, as a dip or sauce in my salmon quiche recipe; maybe kept in refrigerator up to a week.

MEAT MARINADE SAUCE

5 CUPS
Prep Time: 5 minutes Total Time: 24-48 hours

This sauce was inspired to enhance the flavor and moistness to lean cuts of meat such as chicken breast or center cut pork loin chops. This sauce will help seal in the juice and keep the meat from being dried out and tough to the taste. This recipe is very versatile and can be use with any type of meat. If using fish please allow only 24 hours for marinade.

Up to 6 pieces of meat (chicken, pork, fish etc)

4 1/2 Cup of Real Mayonnaise

1/2 Cup red hot chili sauce (Thai) more or less depending on how spicy you like your meat

OR

1/4 Cup chili sauce with any dry rub seasonings (see stuffed chicken recipe under chapter entitled "Meat & Poultry" section for options on dry rubs) or dry ranch dressing mix, dry zesty Italian dressing mix etc; The dry seasoning options are endless depending on what taste you are after (savory, sweet, spicy)

If using dry seasonings rub for meat or with ever seasonings you choose then put into a gallon freezer size zip lock bag, along with mayonnaise and chili sauce; massage the meat so the mixture is fully incorporated and meat is well coated, about 2-3 minutes. Place into refrigerator for minimum of 24 hours to 48 hours (the longer the meat is in marinade the more the meat can absorb the flavors you are after; well worth the time). Once a day take out and massage meat/marinade for about one minute so to incorporate the settled marinade and coat the meat thoroughly and put the meat marinade back into the refrigerator for the remaining time.

Take meat out of gallon freezer bag and discard all meat marinade. Grill your meat or bake in the oven for a succulent piece of meat you have ever tasted before.

NOTES: *Best marinade I have ever had on a lean piece of meat. I always make more than is needed to have throughout the week in other recipes.*

I was first introduced to baking when I was about 10 years old when I made my first M & M chocolate cake (back then no one had ever seen or even heard of this type of cake). I then took it to a cake auction to be auctioned off for some dollar amount. To my surprise my cake caught the highest bid for charity. I thought no one would want a cake made by a 10 year old and my thought was wrong. That is when I knew I had a gift for making baked goods. I then found my way into cooking by helping the older women in my community to clean their homes and in return they shared their recipes for their most intimate home cooked meals with me. So as a result of all this I was led to many different and unique ways of baking and cooking. So throughout my life cooking became a hobby such as doing banquets, wedding parties, family reunions for those I loved as a hobby because I liked making people happy with my cooking and of course all my baked goods. So now I have retired from my day job and with all my free time I was able to go back to my hobby of cooking and baking to my heart was content. I love to volunteer and make a difference through charity. This is how I came to writing a cookbook and using my talents I have developed for the good of others in more ways than just cooking. So all of the proceeds from the sales of this cookbook are going to a charity near and dear to my heart. I wish you all a success in your dreams of cooking and baking as I have done.

INDEX

INDEX

INDEX

INDEX

INDEX

Made in the USA
Charleston, SC
24 May 2011